The Research Report Series of the Institute for Social Research is composed of significant reports published at the completion of a research project. These reports are generally prepared by the principal research investigators and are directed to selected users of this information. Research Reports are intended as technical documents which provide rapid dissemination of new knowledge resulting from ISR research.

RESEARCH REPORT SERIES, INSTITUTE FOR SOCIAL RESEARCH

Career Change in Midlife: Stress, Social Support, and Adjustment

John R. P. French, Jr.
Steven R. Doehrman
Mary Lou Davis-Sacks
Amiram Vinokur

Research Center for Group Dynamics
Institute for Social Research
The University of Michigan
1983

The research described in this report was sponsored in part by the Organizational Effectiveness Research Program, Office of Naval Research (Code 452), under Contract No. N00014-78-0399, NR170-868.

Library of Congress Cataloging in Publication Data: Catalog Card No. 83-18643

ISR Book No. 9018

Published in 1983 by:
Institute for Social Research,
The University of Michigan, Ann Arbor, Michigan

6 5 4 3 2

Manufactured in the United States of America

[redacted]

TABLE OF CONTENTS

LIST OF TABLES

LIST OF FIGURES

ACKNOWLEDGEMENTS

This research project was conducted by the Institute for Social Research at the University of Michigan in close collaboration with the Naval Health Research Center in San Diego. We wish to thank many people in San Diego for consulting help, for making arrangements, for conducting preliminary interviews with 23 Navy retirees and their wives, and for pre-testing the resulting questionnaire. For this advice and assistance we are grateful to Eric Gunderson, James LaRocco, Ross Vickers, Harold Ward, J.H. Atkinson, Martin Cary, Margaret Hanley, Thomas O'Shea, Professor George Drops, and others.

We thank our colleagues in Michigan for the collection, management and analysis of the questionnaire data. Nancy Burks provided expert analysis, Christine Hart coordinated the data collection, and Cheryl Slay prepared the tables and appendices. We are especially grateful to Mary Jo Griewahn for the word processing and a variety of other services.

CAREER CHANGE IN MIDLIFE:

STRESS, SOCIAL SUPPORT, AND ADJUSTMENT

CHAPTER I

INTRODUCTION

The research project described in this report grows out of a program of research at the Institute for Social Research, University of Michigan, which, during the past two decades, has been studying the effects of the social environment on adjustment and health. It continues the focus on organizational stress and individual strain and it also examines how family stresses and social support affect the adjustment of enlisted men who are undergoing a stressful life event-leaving the Navy after twenty years of service and returning to civilian life. The central theoretical approach is the theory of person-environment fit as developed in several of our recent publications (French, et al., 1974; Caplan, et al., 1975; Harrison, 1977; French, et al., 1982).

There are five main objectives of this project.

(1) The first theoretical objective is to extend the study of a general model of personal adjustment conceived as the goodness of fit between the person and his environment by providing a longitudinal test of the hypotheses. We will examine the effects of various dimensions of misfit on a variety of strains such as job dissatisfaction, marital dissatisfaction, anxiety, depression, somatic complaints and low self-esteem.

(2) A second theoretical objective is to extend our findings on social support in relation to stress and strain (Caplan, et al., 1975; Cobb, 1976; House & Wells, 1978; LaRocco, et al., 1980; House, 1981) by applying the theory of person-environment fit to social support. This assumes that a person can suffer from too little social support and also, in certain circumstances, from too much social support.

(3) A third objective is to develop hypotheses and measures about coping and defense as applied to a concrete life stress, i.e.,

leaving the Navy after twenty years of service. Here again person-environment fit theory is used to generate concepts and hypotheses about coping and adjustment.

(4) A fourth objective is practical: to improve our understanding and prediction of retention/attrition by the application of the above theories of person-environment fit, of social support, and of stress and strain.

(5) A fifth objective is to study the chronic and acute stresses involved in career change and to determine the effects of these stresses on a variety of strains.

The design for achieving these objectives compared a group of men who were leaving active service to join the fleet reserve with a control group of enlisted men who stayed in the Navy after twenty years of service. We refer to the former group as "leavers" rather than retirees because they were changing careers in midstream rather than retiring from a full-time job. The leavers and their wives filled out questionnaires at three points in time: one month before leaving the Navy, one month after leaving, and five months later. The control group of "stayers" filled out a similar questionnaire at two points in time separated by six months.

In the next chapter we present the theory of person-environment fit as a general model for the whole project including the major topics of stress and strain, social support, retirement, and coping and defense. More specific statements of hypotheses regarding these topics are reserved for later chapters. After describing the research methods in Chapter III, we proceed in the next three chapters to present the hypotheses and findings on the above major topics. Chapter VII summarizes the main theoretical findings and gives several suggestions for future research.

CHAPTER II

THEORY

This chapter describes briefly three focal theoretical topics which deal primarily with the independent variables: (1) The person-environment fit model of stress; (2) The processes of coping and defense; (3) The role of social support in adjustment to stress. A fourth section deals with the dependent variables of strain, health, and attrition/retention.

The Person-Environment Fit Model

One aim of this project is to test part of a specific model which addresses the effects of acute stress produced by major life events and the effects of chronic stresses in producing strain and illness. By chronic stress we mean a generally high level of some threatening environmental variable (stressor) or a chronic misfit between the stressor and the characteristics of the person. By acute stress we mean a rather sudden increase in an environmental stressor or in the misfit between the person and his environment. As we shall see later, some of our hypotheses and analyses focus on the level of stress and others with the change in this level.

The basic theoretical model is presented in schematic form in Figure II-1. Each numbered arrow running from cause to effect represents a _set of hypotheses_ because each box in the figure contains a number of variables. For example, Hypothesis 1 asserts that several types of _subjective_ job stress will produce several forms of psychological and behavioral strain. However, we expect that no particular stress will affect _all_ forms of strain, and no particular strain will be affected by _all_ forms of stress; instead we expect a certain degree of specificity in the effects of stress on strain. For example, work overload may strongly affect job dissatisfaction but have little or no effect on marital dissatisfaction. There may be several reasons for such patterning of specific results within a general hypothesis, but one general reason we have referred to as the _principle of relevance_. The more _relevant_ a dependent variable is to an

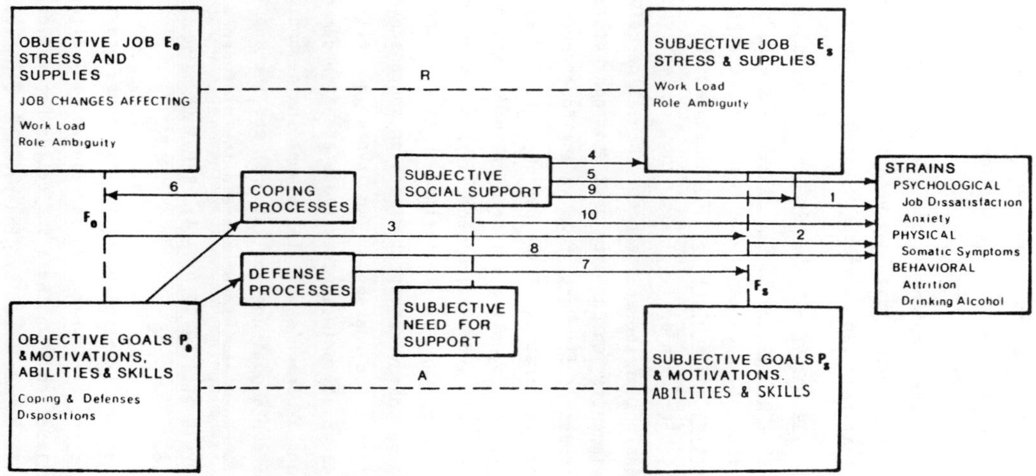

Figure II-1. A model for the effects of job changes on subjective stresses and on strains. The arrows represent causal relations running from cause to effect; an arrow terminating on a second arrow represents a conditioning effect which modifies the causal relations denoted by the second arrow. Broken lines represent discrepancy scores which measure objective fit (F_o), subjective fit (F_s), reality contact (R), and accessibility to self (A). An arrow terminating on a broken line represents causal influence on that discrepancy score. Numbers refer to the hypotheses discussed in the text.

independent variable the more strongly the dependent variable will be affected. By relevance we mean that the two variables refer to the same or similar domains, as in the above example, or that within a single domain the independent and dependent variables refer to the same or similar dimensions. In the job domain, for example, we have found that excess work load has more effect on work load dissatisfaction than on general job dissatisfaction (French, et al., 1982). The maximum relevance would occur, as in this example, where both the independent and the dependent variables refer to the same dimension (work load) and here the two variables are commensurate in the sense that they can be measured using the same scale.

The major purpose of the model is to define quantitatively the adjustment of a person as the goodness of fit between the person and the environment. For each of these two concepts we make a metatheoretical distinction between objective and subjective. For example, the objective person includes objective traits such as I.Q. and the subjective person includes commensurate dimensions of the self concept such as perceived I.Q. Thus four fundamental elements, which are used to generate the two quantitative scores on goodness of fit, are shown in the four square boxes of Figure II-1: (a) objective measures of the person (P_o); (b) subjective measures of the person (P_s); (c) objective measures of the environment (E_o) and (d) subjective measures of the environment (E_s). Objective fit, represented by a vertical broken line labelled F_o, is defined as the difference between a score on an environmental dimension and a score on a commensurate dimension of the person. Two types of fit can be distinguished: (1) The discrepancy between the stress of a job demand such as a heavy work load and a person's ability to meet the demand; (2) The discrepancy between the person's goal (or motivations) and the supplies in the environment to satisfy these goals, for example the difference between a man's desire for high levels of job complexity minus a low level of complexity in his actual job.

Corresponding to these two types of objective fit there are two types of subjective person-environment fit which are represented in Figure II-1 by a vertical broken line labelled F_s. These subjective perceptions of the job and of the person are measured by the person's own report in an interview or a questionnaire.

Arrow 1 in Figure II-1 denotes the major hypothesis that subjective stress (E_s) influences strain. Arrow 2 represents the parallel hypothesis that subjective person-environment fit also influences strain. Although it is not shown in Figure II-1, it is also hypothesized that person-environment fit will account for additional variance in strain, over and above that accounted for by E_s and P_s.

The objective variables in Figure II-1 (E_o, P_o and F_o) are not shown as having direct effects on our dependent strains partly because our general hypothesis states that the effects of the objective variables on these strains will generally be mediated by the corresponding subjective variables. For example, objective fit will affect subjective fit (see Arrow 3 in Figure II-1) which in turn will affect strains. In addition we do not have good objective measures in this project and therefore the hypotheses about objective predictors cannot be tested. Nevertheless, they are included in the basic model because the interpretation of the results and the suggestions for applying the findings may often involve these objective variables. In general, perception tends to be veridical, although biases do occur; so E_s will generally correlate highly with E_o.

An objective job stress, such as high role ambiguity on a job, may be denied or distorted by the person as a way of reducing subjective misfit. However, such defensive denial will reduce reality contact, R, as measured by the difference between the objective and the subjective ambiguity (see the top broken line in Figure II-1). On the other hand, the person may magnify his own evaluation of his abilities as another way of reducing subjective misfit. This defensive maneuver will reduce accessibility of the self, A, as measured by the discrepancy on commensurate measures of objective and subjective ability (see the bottom broken line in Figure II-1). These four discrepancy scores F_o, F_s, R, and A (the four main broken lines in Figure II-1) define four important conceptions of mental health. In this model they form a dynamic system in the sense that a change in any one of them will necessarily produce a change in at least one other. Furthermore, the magnitude of these quantitative changes can be deduced from the model. Just as defensive distortions of one's job or of one's self may improve subjective fit, so the converse realistic perception of an objective misfit may produce subjective misfit which will lead, according to Hypothesis 2, to psychological and behavioral strain. Thus realistic perceptions, which are often considered a criterion of good mental health, may lead to bad mental health when the person cannot cope successfully with an objective misfit. Under these circumstances, an undermining of the person's defenses will, according to this model, have undesirable consequences. On the other hand, unrealistic perceptions of one's job and of one's self and of the goodness of fit between the two may also lead to inappropriate actions which make the objective situation worse. For example, the man who projects the blame for his poor performance onto his superior may get fired. These feedback loops are not shown in Figure II-1, but their effects must be taken into account in any complete theory of adjustment to stress. Clearly we will not have a good understanding of the effects of stress until we have a good knowledge of how people cope with stress and defend against stress and strain.

Coping and Defense

Most earlier work has considered coping and defensive reactions to be operative primarily during adjustment to stressful situations, which are either intrapsychic or extrapsychic in origin. Generally, coping has been defined as attempts by the person to change the objective aspects of himself or of the environment whereas defenses pertain to changes in the subjective aspects of the person or situation. We define defenses as changes in the subjective situation (E_s and P_s) without corresponding changes in E_o and P_o. By definition, therefore, defenses involve distortion.

As Hypothesis 6 suggests, coping is concerned with improving objective fit by altering the objective facts: either the objective environment and/or the objective person are changed in such a way as to reduce objective misfit. For example, a person who is overloaded by a new job might ask for a reduced work load ("environmental mastery") and/or might take special training to increase his ability to handle the work ("adaptation to the environment"). In a parallel fashion, Hypothesis 7 asserts that defense processes are concerned with reducing subjective misfit by altering either the subjective environment or the subjective self without corresponding changes in the objective facts. For example, "denial of overload" (Vickers, 1979) measures an under-estimation of the work load, a response which improves the subjective fit of a man who is overloaded.

In developing our theory and measures of both coping and defense we distinguished processes from dispositions. For example, the process of coping with overload by the overt behavior of going to the boss and asking for a reduction in work load is different from the disposition to use this form of environmental mastery. We have measures of only the generalized dispositions, but we hypothesize that these dispositions will lead to the utilization of the corresponding processes which in turn will lead to reductions in objective misfit (for coping) or of subjective misfit (for defenses) as shown in Figure II-1.

Coping and defense processes are here defined as "efforts directed toward changing elements of adjustment" rather than "changes in elements of adjustment." The classification system presented in Table II-1 defines and classifies coping and defense processes according to the element of adjustment toward which the processes are directed. Coping processes are defined as efforts directed toward changing objective elements of adjustment. Defense processes are defined as efforts directed toward changing subjective elements of adjustment or affective responses rather than changing objective elements of adjustment. Four categories of coping processes are generated based on the four objective fit elements: efforts directed toward changing objective environmental demands, objective environmental supplies, objective motives of the person, and objective abilities of the person. Similarly, four categories of defense processes are generated based on the four subjective fit elements: efforts directed toward changing subjective environmental demands, subjective environmental supplies, subjective motives of the person, subjective abilities of the person without changing the corresponding objective factors. Each of these categories can be further divided into two subcategories: efforts directed toward increasing the element of adjustment and efforts directed toward decreasing the element of adjustment. Hence, the classification system presented here identifies sixteen specific categories of coping and defense processes.

It is assumed that coping and defense processes are learned behaviors. More specifically, it is assumed that an individual who has been reinforced for using a particular coping or defense process is more likely to use this process in subsequent situations to the extent that the person perceives the subsequent situation to be similar, on a set of critical dimensions, to the situation in which he/she was previously reinforced. At present, we can only speculate as to which dimensions will be critical for any given individual.

Disposition refers to the tendency of the person to engage in a coping or defense process. The strength and situational specificity of coping and defense dispositions reflect past schedules of reinforcement. We attempted to measure coping and defense dispositions using a vignette format. Six vignettes were presented. All described stressful situations likely to be encountered in the transition from Navy to civilian life.

Table II-1

Classification System of Coping and Defense Processes[a]

I. Coping Processes (directed toward objective environment and/or person)

A. Mastery Processes (directed toward objective environmental supplies and/or demands)

1. Mastery of Environmental Demands
   a. Mastery of Environmental Demands Upward
   b. Mastery of Environmental Demands Downward

2. Mastery of Environmental Supplies
   a. Mastery of Environmental Supplies Upward
   b. Mastery of Environmental Supplies Downward

B. Adaptation Processes (directed toward objective motives and/or abilities of person)

1. Adaptation of Motives
   a. Adaptation of Motives Upward
   b. Adaptation of Motives Downward

2. Adaptation of Abilities
   a. Adaptation of Abilities Upward
   b. Adaptation of Abilities Downward

II. Defense Processes (directed toward subjective environment and/or person)

A. Distortion Processes (directed toward subjective environmental supplies and/or demands)

1. Distortion of Environmental Demands
   a. Distortion of Environmental Demands Upward
   b. Distortion of Environmental Demands Downward

2. Distortion of Environmental Supplies
   a. Distortion of Environmental Supplies Upward
   b. Distortion of Environmental Suppies Downward

B. Re-assessment Processes (directed toward subjective motives and/or abilities of person)

1. Re-assessment of Motives
   a. Re-assessment of Motives Upward
   b. Re-assessment of Motives Downward

2. Re-assessment of Abilities
   a. Re-assessment of Abilities Upward
   b. Re-assessment of Abilities Downward

[a]All processes listed under Roman numeral I are coping processes. All processes listed under Roman numeral II are defense processes. Major categories of coping and defense processes are identified by capitalized letters. Within each category, sub-groups of processes are ideitnfied by Arabic numerals. Specific processes within each sub-group are identified by non-capitalized letters.

Following each vignette, respondents were asked to indicate the probability that they would engage in coping and defense processes. The low internal consistency, stability, and predictive validity of these measures prevented us from employing them in tests of our hypotheses. The measures might have been stronger had they been specific to commonly experienced stresses with longer histories of reinforcement.

The Role of Social Support in Adjustment to Stress

Social support is extremely important during acute stresses such as in career change and retirement. Typically, leaving a job means leaving several major sources of social support such as one's supervisor and one's peers. The importance of social support in promoting retention in the Navy is indicated by a study conducted by the Institute for Social Research (Drexler & Bowers, 1973). In aggregate data from 22 ships the correlations between total re-enlistment rate and social support from supervisor, peers, and the organization were .40, .39, and .33 respectively.

In testing hypotheses about the effects of social support we will again be testing the same general model of person-environment fit. The variables of subjective support, subjective need for support, and the difference score between the two (i.e., fit with respect to social support) will be examined for both main effects and interaction effects. We predict that subjective social support will reduce stress (arrow 4 in Figure II-1), will reduce strain (arrow 5) and will buffer the effect of stress on strain (arrow 9). We also predict that fit with respect to social support will predict additional variance in strain over and above the additive effects of subjective support and the subjective need for support. More detailed hypotheses and findings are presented in Chapter V.

The Dependent Variables

The rationale for selecting certain measures of strain, of mental health, and of physical health has been presented elsewhere (French & Kahn, 1962; Caplan, et al., 1975), but the reasons for focussing on retention/attrition in this study should be discussed. The importance of the practical problem is clear: high rates of attrition entail high costs of recruiting, selecting, and training; they result in a Navy with less experience, lower efficiency and poorer performance; and they greatly increase the already burdensome costs of pensions and benefits. The theoretical reasons for studying retention/attrition in this particular project stem from the project's focus on social support, person-environment fit and coping and defense. In a wide variety of settings it has been shown that social support from others in the setting is an important force keeping people in that setting (Caplan, et al., 1976, p. 45). For example, 19 studies in medical settings show that social support from health practictioners is a factor in preventing patients from dropping out of treatment (Baekeland & Lundwall, 1975). More relevant for present purposes are the findings cited earlier showing that retention in the Navy is substantially correlated with social support from supervisors, coworkers, and the organization.

The theoretical reasons for linking retention to person-environment fit are more cogent, but the evidence is more indirect. It is hypothesized that a man will be motivated to leave an environment which does not satisfy his needs and which makes demands which he cannot meet, provided only that some better fitting environment is available to him. We already know that environmental variables, such as leadership and organizational climate, are substantially related to retention in the Navy (Drexler & Bowers, 1973). Further, we believe that goodness of fit with respect to these environmental variables should contribute to better predictions of strain than have their component parts (Caplan, et al., 1975; French, et al., 1982; Harrison, 1976; Harrison, 1977).

Finally, we shall be testing the very plausible hypothesis that a variety of other strains in Navy life will contribute to a man's decision to leave the Navy. Although this hypothesis has been omitted from Figure II-1, it is examined in some detail in Chapter VI.

In summary, we can now point out that the person-environment fit model provides some integration across such diverse topics as stress and strain, social support, coping, defense, and attrition. The same basic model generates both the basic concepts and the major hypotheses about these topics as shown in Figure II-1.

CHAPTER III

METHODS

Design

The study consisted of two phases: an initial, pilot phase for instrument development and a second, main phase providing data to test hypotheses and research questions growing out of the theoretical model presented in Chapter II. The pilot phase utilized interviews and questionnaires obtained from twenty year Navy enlisted men who had decided to leave the Navy. Home interviews in the San Diego, California area were conducted in order to yield case material that generated many of the vignettes and reactions for the coping and defense scales discussed in Chapter II. Pilot questionnaire data were collected from these interviewees and from men attending Navy preretirement workshops, sponsored by National University of San Diego and led by Professor George Drops. These preliminary findings were used to adapt measures from our earlier research at the Institute for Social Research to our sample of Navy enlisted men.

The main phase of the study collected longitudinal, questionnaire data from two groups of enlisted men: leavers who voluntarily left the Navy after 20-22 years of service, and stayers who remained in the Navy for at least one more enlistment period after 20-22 years of service.

Data were collected from the leavers at three points in time and from the stayers at two times. This longitudinal design provided data for the longitudinal testing of hypotheses. The stayers served as a comparison group for testing hypotheses about why one group decided to leave the Navy whereas the other group decided to stay. The decision to leave the Navy is explored in detail in Chapter VI. Data were collected from the leavers one month before leaving, one month after leaving, and six months after leaving. The two data collection times for the stayers differed from each other by six months.

The data collection process extended over 18 months, from September of 1979 until March of 1981. The questionnaire of the leavers was altered in February of 1980 resulting in, for some measures, two groups of leavers - an 'early' group of leavers and a 'later' group of leavers. Also, data collection from the stayers was initiated in April of 1980, seven months after it was began for the leavers.

In addition to obtaining data from Navy enlisted men, we also collected data from many of their wives. This information was useful in providing quasi-objective measures of the stress and social support of the men in the home environment.

Subjects

The criteria for inclusion in the study were as follows: 1.) Navy enlisted men with twenty to twenty two years of service, 2.) in good standing with the Navy, 3.) married. The subjects were located throughout the world at ship and shore stations.

We studied men with at least 20 years of service because Navy personnel are first eligible to leave the Navy and receive a pension at that point. They are considered to be on reserve status until 30 years from their initial enlistment date. The longer a man stays in after 20 years the greater are his pension benefits, up to a maximum for 30 years of service.

The leavers were sent the first of three mailings four to six weeks prior to their voluntary separation date from the Navy. The initial mailing, which included the first questionnaire, was directed to their work location and constituted their first contact with our study. A cover letter served to recruit the man to become a participant in the study, to describe the purpose of the study, and to explain the details of our expectations of the subjects. A sample cover letter and accompanying information sheet appear in Appendix A.

For the stayers, the initial mailing explained the purpose of the study and inquired as to the man's intention to remain in the Navy beyond the twenty to twenty two years he had already served. We subsequently sent questionnaires to those men who indicated they intended to reenlist after the current enlistment was over, even if they were uncertain about staying in the Navy for thirty years.

The first two months of initial mailings to leavers, i.e., during September and October of 1979, produced a return rate for completed questionnaires of only 17.5% of those mailed. This extremely low response rate proved costly and time consuming. Instead of collecting time one data over a three month period, as originally planned, it was necessary to extend time one data collection for an extra six months.

In order to improve our rate of return, we introduced two experimental manipulations for the November, 1979 mailings. In a 2x2 design, we sent the initial mailing via certified mail and/or we included a token incentive payment of a silver dollar. The results, reported in detail in our ONR Technical Report I-1 (French and Doehrman, 1980), are summarized in Table III-1. The data show that the incentive payment more than doubled the return rate to 34.5%. In subsequent mailings, we always included the incentive payment.

Table III-2 provides information about the number of completed questionnaires that were collected from leavers and stayers at each time of data collection. The frequencies in the table indicate that we have sufficient numbers of subjects for the analyses to be presented in later chapters and that the return rate of later mailings from subjects who had returned the first questionnaire far exceeded the return rate for the first mailing. Note that the second mailing for data from the stayers is labelled 'time three.' This emphasizes that the first and second mailings for data from the stayers are separated almost as long as the first and third mailings for data from the leavers. Hence, in subsequent chapters time three data of stayers is compared with time three data of leavers. As noted above, the initial mailings to stayers began just as initial mailings to leavers had ceased. Hence, data from the leavers were collected an average of about five months earlier in real time than the data collected from stayers.

The low response rate of 34.5% listed in Table III-1 calls into question the representativeness of the sample and limits the generalizability of our findings to the population of twenty year Navy enlisted men. One method of evaluating the representativeness of our subjects is to compare them with nonrespondents. The only information we have for nonrespondents is their pay grade. Table III-3 provides the percentage of returns as a function of pay grade. The higher pay grades, E-8 and E-9, had about twice the return rate as the lower pay grades, E-6 and E-7. Yet, although they are over represented, the two highest pay grades still composed less than one half of the total returns. Thus our sample is not grossly skewed on pay grade although it could conceivably be

Table III-1: Percent of positive responses as a function of the certified mail and incentive payment conditions[1]

	Incentive	No Incentive	Mean
Certified Mail	38.6 (N=57)	15.1 (N=53)	27.3[2]
Not Certified	30.3 (N=56)	18.5 (N=54)	24.5[2]
Mean	34.5[3]	16.8[3]	

[1] Results pertain to the mailings and returns (N=220) during November, 1979 for retirees.

[2] Chi-square = 0.09, N.S. Hence, the return rate did not differ as a function of whether or not the questionnaire was sent via certified mail.

[3] Chi-square = 8.06, p=.01, one-tailed. Hence, the payment of a $1 incentive yielded a significantly greater return rate than the absence of such a payment.

Table III-2: Number of completed questionnaires for leavers and stayers at each time[1]

	Time One	Time Two	Time Three
Leavers	695	525 (75.5)	475 (90.5)
Stayers	217	—	157 (72.4)

[1]Numbers in parentheses indicate the percent return rate for those who returned the previous questionnaire.

Table III-3: Frequency and percentages of mailing and returns as a function of the (potential) respondents' paygrade.[1]

	Paygrade			
	E-6	E-7	E-8	E-9
Number Mailed	184	371	176	96
Number Returned	24	55	40	26
% returns for each paygrade	13.04	14.82	22.73	27.08
% of total mailed	22.25	44.86	21.28	11.61
% of total returns	16.55	37.93	27.59	17.93

[1]Results pertain to mailings and returns (N=145) during September and October, 1979 for leavers.

on some other unknown variable. Hence a measure of caution must be used in generalizing our findings to all twenty year leavers and stayers. It would be even more risky, however, to generalize our findings to men who leave the Navy after only one or two enlistment periods or who are associated with another branch of the Armed Forces.

An issue related to the representativeness of our respondents to the total population concerns dropouts from the study. In a longitudinal design, subjects who fail to complete all the questionnaires may differ from those who do complete all questionnaires. Hence, their absence can distort the findings. Table III-4 presents relevant data for leavers. The table shows the results of t-tests contrasting subsequent responders and dropouts on major variables measured at the preceding data collection time. Seven of 38 t-tests are significant, at $p<.05$. Only pay grade yielded a consistent difference: as in Table III-3, the responders had significantly higher pay grades than the dropouts. However, on four of the five other significant differences between responders and dropouts, the trend of the results is not in the same direction at the two points. Hence, we conclude that the relatively small percentage of subjects who did not complete all of the questionnaires were not sharply different from the continuing subjects on the major variables of interest in the study. Similar analyses for the stayers, not reported here, lead to the same conclusion.

Measures

The measures collected from the men in each condition at each data collection point are listed in Table III-5. The measures are grouped according to theoretical categories discussed in Chapter II. The categories are: Stress, Social Support, Coping, Defense, Strain, Effective Coping, and Demographics. As Table III-5 demonstrates, not all measures were collected from all subjects at each data collection time. In order to shorten the questionnaire, and hopefully to increase the response rate, unnecessary questions were not repeated (e.g., age) and other variables were measured only in the most appropriate group, e.g., coping and defense was measured in leavers. Also, the measure of attitudes toward Navy vs. civilian life was only collected from the early group of leavers, although it was collected from all of the stayers.

The specific items included in each of the measures listed in Table III-5 are provided in Appendix B. Almost all of the items for the measures come from previous research projects within the Social Environment and Health Program at the Institute for Social Research. In general, the mean

Table III-4: Findings of t-tests contrasting subsequent responders and dropouts on major variables measured at the preceding time for leavers

Variables	Time 1 means for time 2 responders (N=525) and dropouts (N=170)		Time 2 means for time 3 responders (N-475) and dropouts (N=50)	
Stresses:	Responders	Dropouts	Responders	Dropouts
Job Complexity E_s	5.64	5.63	5.36	4.95
Job Complexity F^1_s	.29	.40	-.24	-.24
Work Load E_s	3.57	3.53	3.31*	3.56*
Role Ambiguity E_s	1.48**	1.25**	1.11	1.20
Role Ambiguity F^1_s	.49*	.21*	.48	.48
Underutilization of Abilities	1.70	1.63	1.79	2.17
Social Supports:				
Wife E_s	3.67	3.71	3.67	3.67
Supervisor E_s	2.97	3.04	3.41*	2.83*
Strains:				
Anxiety	1.84	1.86	1.62	1.60
Depression	1.56	1.56	1.68	1.58
Irritation	1.62	1.61	1.58	1.68
Somatic Complaints	1.23	1.21	1.25	1.26
Marital Dissatisfaction	1.56	1.52	1.27	1.37
Low Self-esteem	1.24	1.25	1.50	1.51
Job Dissatisfaction	2.54	2.50	1.61	1.56
Effective Coping:				
School	1.29	1.29	1.36	1.43
Work	1.50	1.47	1.65	1.58
Demographics:				
Education	2.93	2.83	2.96**	2.77**
Paygrade	7.17*	7.00*	7.20**	6.97**

**$p < .01$
*$p < .05$

[1] $F_s = E_s - P_s$

Table III-5: Measures collected from subjects in each condition at each time.
(Y=yes, data were collected; N=no, data were not collected.)

	Leavers			Stayers	
Stress:	Time 1	Time 2	Time 3	Time 1	Time 3
Job Complexity (E_s and P_s)	Y	Y	Y	Y	Y
Work Load (E_s and P_s)	Y	Y	Y	Y	Y
Role Ambiguity (E_s and P_s)	Y	Y	Y	Y	Y
Underutilization of Abilities (E_s)	Y	Y	Y	Y	Y
Nontransferability of Skills	N	N	Y	N	N
Inequity of Pay	N	N	Y	N	Y
Marital Stress (E_s and P_s)	Y	Y	Y	Y	Y
Navy vs. Civilian Life	Y[1]	N	N	Y	N
Social Support:					
Supervisor (E_s)	Y	Y	Y	Y	Y
Co-worker (E_s)	Y	N	N	Y	Y
Wife (E_s and P_s)	Y	Y	Y	Y	Y
Coping:					
Mastery Demands	Y	Y	N	N	N
Mastery Supplies	Y	Y	N	N	N
Adaptation Skills	Y	Y	N	N	N
Adaptation Goals	Y	Y	N	N	N
Defense:					
Constriction of Affect	Y	Y	N	N	N
Reversal	Y	Y	N	N	N
Intellectualism	Y	Y	N	N	N

[1] Approximately thirty-seven percent of the leavers at time 1 were tested on this measure.

	Leavers			Stayers	
	Time 1	Time 2	Time 3	Time 1	Time 3
Displacement onto Another	Y	Y	N	N	N
Displacement onto Self	Y	Y	N	N	N
Distorted Locus of Control	Y	Y	N	N	N
Strain:					
Anxiety	Y	Y	Y	Y	Y
Depression	Y	Y	Y	Y	Y
Irritation	Y	Y	Y	Y	Y
Alcohol Use	Y	Y	Y	Y	Y
Obesity	Y	Y	Y	Y	Y
Somatic Complaints	Y	Y	Y	Y	Y
Ill Health	Y	Y	Y	Y	Y
Marital Dissatisfaction	Y	Y	Y	Y	Y
Low Self-esteem	Y	Y	Y	Y	Y
Job Dissatisfaction	Y	Y	Y	Y	Y
Navy Dissatisfaction	Y	N	N	Y	Y
Effective Coping:					
School	Y	Y	Y	N	N
Work	Y	Y	Y	N	N
Demographics:					
Age	Y	N	N	Y	N
Education	Y	N	N	Y	N
Paygrade	Y	N	N	Y	N
Length of Marriage	Y	N	N	Y	N
Number of Children	Y	N	N	Y	N
Supervision of Others	Y	Y	Y	Y	Y
Number Supervised	Y	Y	Y	Y	Y

of each subject's responses to all of the items making up a measure was calculated subsequent to any reverse scoring that may have been necessary. The mean score represented the subject's index on the measure in question and was used in further analyses. Whenever the text refers to a specific measure or index, the first letters of the measure are capitalized. Furthermore, the index is named for the end of the scale with the most stress or strain, such as 'Job Dissatisfaction,' rather than 'Job Satisfaction.'

Cross-sectional reliabilities for each measure, as indicated by coefficient alpha (see Nunnally, 1967), are provided in Table III-6. The reliabilities range from fair to good. The alphas for the job stress measures are not as high as in previous studies which collected data from stably employed men. Perhaps the transitory nature of the men's jobs one month before Navy separation adversely affected the cross-sectional reliability. It is noteworthy that the social support and strain measures, which perhaps were more salient to the men at the time, showed appreciably higher reliabilities.

The stability of each measure was determined by correlating each leaver's index at time one with his index at time two. The duration between time one and time two was about two months. During that time the men left the Navy, perhaps moved from one home to another, and most likely either began school or started a new job. Hence it was not appropriate to calculate stability for those measures with a different referent at time two than at time one, e.g., job stress measures. For measures with the same referent at the two times, e.g., social support from the wife or the man's anxiety, the issue arises as to whether the measure assesses a general, enduring characteristic of the person or a specific, perhaps temporary, attribute of the person. The former would be expected to have higher stabilities than the latter. Cognitive and behavioral measures generally assess more enduring and less volatile characteristics than affective measures. This supposition is borne out in Table III-6 in which the affective strains have stabilities around .40 whereas the cognitive and behavioral strains are generally much higher, .49-.79. Those measures which involve social relationships, namely social support and marital stress, have stabilities in the .40-.60 range. Health measures have a range from .51 to .66. Perhaps the most striking aspect of the measures of stability in Table III-6 is their overall high value given the many life changes that occurred between the two data collection times.

Table III-6

Coefficient alpha at time 1 for measures collected from 435 leavers. Stability coefficients between time 1 and time 2 for 520 leavers.[a]

Measure	Number of items	Coefficient alpha	Stability[c]
Stress:			
Job complexity, E_s	3	.63	
Job complexity, P_s	3	.67	
Job complexity, $F^b{}_s$	3	.59	
Work Load, E_s	4	.75	
Work Load, P_s	4	.40	
Work Load, , $F^b{}_s$	4	.79	
Role Ambiguity, E_s	3	.81	
Role Ambiguity, P_s	3	.85	
Role Ambiguity, $F^b{}_s$	3	.84	
Underutilization of Abilities	2	.49	
Marital Stress, E_s	3	.49	.47
Marital Stress, P_s	3	.65	.45
Marital Stress, $F^b{}_s$	3	.56	.40
Social Support			
Supervisor	3	.87	
Wife, E_s	6	.93	.65
Wife, P_s	6	.88	.43
Wife, $F^b{}_s$	6	.87	.54

Strain:	Number of items	Coefficient alpha	Stability
Anxiety	4	.80	.34
Depression	6	.86	.41
Irritation	4	.87	.37
Alcohol Use	3	.85	.79
Obesity	1		.60
Somatic Complaints	10	.76	.51
Ill Health	1		.66
Marital Dissatisfaction	6	.89	.75
Low Self-esteem	3	.70	.49
Job Dissatisfaction	3	.82	
Navy Dissatisfaction	3	.75	
Effective Coping:			
School	7	.76	.64
Work	7	.76	.57

[a]The reliabilities and stabilities of coping and defense measures are presented in Chapter VII.

[b]$F_s = E_s - P_s$

[c]Values are not provided for those measures which pertain to different situations at the two times.

Appendices C and D present the zero-order product moment correlations for all the major measures collected from the leavers at time one and from the stayers at time one, respectively.

Methods of Analysis

On several occasions in subsequent chapters results of multiple regression analyses will be presented. The statistical program that was used gives two outputs: the partial correlation of each predictor variable with the dependent variable and the unstandardized regression coefficient for each predictor. The particular output that is presented in subsequent chapters will be determined by the purposes of the analyses at hand.

Three types of regression analyses were performed: regular regressions, forward regressions and ordered regressions. Regular regressions entail determining the contribution of each predictor variable to the dependent variable holding constant the remaining predictor variables. Forward and ordered regressions differ from the regular regressions according to the manner in which the predictor variables are added to the regression equation. With forward regressions the program selects among predictors in the order that they account for variance in the dependent variable, that which accounts for the most variance coming first. The process continues as long as there are predictors which account for a significant amount of variance. With ordered regressions, the program selects among predictors in the order specified beforehand with the process continuing until the list is exhausted. Typically, theoretical hypotheses specify the order of predictors for ordered regressions. This is not the case for forward regressions that involve a comparison of predictors in an empirical fashion. Subsequent chapters will clarify how the different regression analyses are suitable for evaluating the various hypotheses.

The remaining complex statistical procedure employed in the study was path analysis. Details of this technique will be given in Chapter VI.

Suitability of the Measures for Testing P-E Fit Theory

In order to test the various hypotheses pertaining to P-E fit theory it is first necessary to determine if the relevant measures are appropriate for the task (see also French, et al., 1982, Chapter III). Three aspects of the measures of fit must be considered. First, the correlation between P_s and E_s should not be so high that fit or difference scores have a narrow range that would reduce correlations with strains. Second, the variances of P_s and E_s should not be so discrepant that one or the other index is primarily responsible for variation in fit scores. And third, the distribution of (E-P) should extend on both sides of zero so that the theoretical curves relating fit measures of stress with strain can receive adequate empirical testing.

The data in Table III-7 present the correlations between E_s and P_s for the four measures of fit used in the study. None of the correlations are so high that the spread of fit scores would be greatly restricted.

Table III-8 provides the means and standard deviations of E_s and P_s for the four measures of fit. At each point in time the standard deviations of the two components of fit on job complexity, role ambiguity and marital stress are quite similar. The standard deviation of wife social support E_s is, in general, about a third larger than that of wife social support P_s. In sum, E_s contributes somewhat more than P_s to fit scores for wife social support whereas both contribute equally to fit scores of Job Complexity, Role Ambiguity, and Marital Stress.

Tables III-9 presents the distributions on the fit variable (E-P) for each measure. The table lists the percentage of scores within different standard deviations on either side of perfect fit (E-P=0). All of the measures show distributions on both sides of perfect fit; that is, a substantial number of men report too much of an environmental variable and a substantial number of other men report too little of this same variable. With these distributions the relevant hypotheses can be tested.

<u>Four Different Ways to Calculate Fit</u>.

In Table III-9 one formula for calculating fit, (E-P) or the arithmetic difference between E_s and P_s, is indicated. This measure of fit is termed 'Good Fit.' Scores on either side of perfect fit (where E-P=0) are instances of misfit. For example, if a man has job complexity of +4 (E_s) and desires job complexity of +2 (P_s), his good fit score would be a misfit of +2. But if the man has job complexity of +2 (E) and wants a complexity of +4 (P_s), his good fit score would be a misfit of -2. Both examples involve misfits, one of too much complexity and the other of too little complexity.

A second fit score, termed 'Poor Fit', considers only the absolute value of the difference between E_s and P_s. I.e., poor fit is defined as equal to $|E_s-P_s|$ disregarding the sign of the difference.

A third way to calculate fit results in a score of "Deficiency Fit." Here, all cases where P_s is less than E_s are set at perfect fit or E-P=0.

Table III-7. Correlations between E_s and P_s for the fit measures at each time for leavers

Measure	Time 1	Time 2	Time 3
Job Complexity	.31	.58	.48
Role Ambiguity	.06	.28	.30
Marital Stress	.50	.44	.46
Wife Social Support	.38	.35	.41

Table III-8. Means and standard deviations of E_s and P_s for the fit measures of leavers at each time.

	Time 1				Time 2				Time 3			
	E		P		E		P		E		P	
	$\bar{x}$	S.D.	$\bar{x}$	S.D	$\bar{x}$	S.D.	$\bar{x}$	S.D.	$\bar{x}$	S.D.	$\bar{x}$	S.D.
Job Complexity	5.64	1.04	5.31	1.09	5.31	1.24	5.46	1.12	5.25	1.12	5.34	1.03
Role Ambiguity	2.43	1.00	2.00	1.11	2.12	1.00	1.64	.90	2.09	.89	1.61	.82
Marital Stress	3.53	.66	3.64	.74	3.52	.68	3.71	.70	3.45	.68	3.64	.65
Wife Social Support	3.68	.98	3.82	.72	3.67	.92	3.67	.73	3.66	.87	3.72	.65

Table III-9. Distributions on the fit variable (E-P) for each measure in terms of percentages for each standard deviation on either side of perfect fit (E-P=0).

Measure[1]	-3 or less	-2	-1	0	+1	+2	+3 or more	S.D. on original scale
Job Complexity$_1$	0.9	3.4	14.9	42.9	25.9	10.0	2.0	1.25
Job Complexity$_2$	2.5	4.8	20.8	54.2	12.4	3.8	1.5	1.08
Job Complexity$_3$	2.3	4.9	15.7	56.3	15.7	4.2	1.0	1.10
Role Ambiguity$_1$	0.4	5.6	10.5	43.4	29.5	9.2	1.3	1.45
Role Ambiguity$_2$	0.8	2.3	10.3	41.3	35.8	6.0	3.5	1.15
Role Ambiguity$_3$	1.4	1.6	7.4	42.1	34.7	9.4	3.5	1.02
Marital Stress$_1$	1.3	3.8	19.9	58.5	13.3	1.8	1.3	.70
Marital Stress$_2$	2.0	5.1	23.6	53.7	13.0	1.6	1.0	.73
Marital Stress$_2$	2.2	5.0	21.0	56.6	12.8	2.0	0.4	.69
Wife Social Support$_1$	3.7	6.7	17.3	46.8	22.0	3.2	0.3	.97
Wife Social Support$_2$	2.0	3.3	20.7	44.9	24.0	4.1	1.0	.96
Wife Social Support$_3$	1.7	6.3	17.4	50.0	19.8	3.5	1.3	.85

[1]Subscripts refer to time of data collection. Subjects are leavers.

Cases where P_s is greater than E_s are those where there is a deficiency in E_s.

The fourth fit score is termed "Excess Fit." In this instance, cases where P_s is greater than E_s are set at zero. Cases where E_s is greater than P_s are those where there is an excess of E_s.

Chapter IV takes up the question of whether the four different fit scores for stress have different effects on strain. Chapter V examines a similar question about fit with respect to social support.

CHAPTER IV

THE EFFECTS OF STRESS ON STRAIN

Hypotheses and Research Questions.

This chapter is concerned with the effects of stress on strain, with the testing of specific hypotheses elaborating on the general hypotheses outlined in Chapter II and also with certain research questions about stress and strain which do not derive directly from person-environment fit theory but which do often deal with the replication of previous empirical findings about stress and strain. We start with a statement of these hypotheses and research questions.

Hypothesis la: The greater the environmental stress the greater the strain. The major environmental stresses, E_s, include: Job Complexity, Work Load, Role Ambiguity, Underutilization of Abilities, and Marital Stress. The major strains include: Marital Dissatisfaction, Anxiety, Depression, Irritation, Somatic Complaints, Low Self-esteem, and Job Dissatisfaction. All of these measures are described in Chapter III.

Hypothesis la can be tested in two different fashions. First, a cross-sectional analysis would determine if the level of stress at a given time is related to the level of strain at the same time. Such an analysis would indicate a relationship between the two variables but without specifying the direction of causality. A second method considers the relation between the level of stress at one time with the level of strain at a subsequent time. This approach tests the direction of causality but does not distinguish the effects of chronic stress from the effects of acute stress. Either type of stress could produce consequent strain. Question 3 below deals with this issue.

Hypothesis lb: Moving one's residence during the time of retirement from the Navy is an additional stress which will add to the strain.

Hypothesis 1c: The lower the transferability of job skills from the Navy job to civilian jobs the greater the strain.

Hypothesis 2a: Misfit between the person and his environment will explain additional variance in strain, over and above the additive effects of its components, E_s, and P_s.

Hypothesis 2b: The worse the fit between the person and his environment, the greater the strain.

Question 1: Do different forms of misfit (as measured by different indices, i.e., Good Fit, Poor Fit, Deficiency Fit, Excess Fit) have different effects on strains? Are there meaningful patterns in these relationships?

Question 2: We expect a certain amount of specificity in the effects of stress on strain. Can we replicate the specific relations found in French et al., 1982: a. Job Complexity - Poor Fit and Underutilization of Abilities influence Job Dissatisfaction; b. Does Underutilization also influence irritation?

Hypotheses 1b and 1c and Question 2 all involve specific instances of the more general Hypothesis 1a. Hypotheses 1b and 1c concern stresses peculiar to men changing residences or jobs whereas Question 2 focuses upon stress-strain relations previously found in a stably employed sample.

Hypotheses 2a and 2b deal with important predictions of Person-Environment Fit Theory about the added explanatory power that is contributed when the person's desires are considered along with the person's perceptions of environmental stresses.

Hypothesis 3: The greater the relevance of the dependent strain to the environmental stress, E_s or F_s, the greater the effect of the stress on this strain.

Question 3: Can we distinguish the effects of acute stress from those of chronic stress? Will the rate of <u>increase</u> in stress account for additional variance in subsequent strain beyond that accounted for by the final level of stress?

Whereas Hypothesis 1a deals with the <u>levels</u> of the independent variable (stress) and the dependent variable (strain), Question 3 pertains to <u>changes</u> in stress and strain over time. Since both variables are measured over the same time interval neither is antecedent to the other and the direction of causality cannot be ascertained. So we tested Question 3 with a multiple regression analysis which operationalized change in strain by predicting to strain at time 3 after controlling for strain at time 2. The change in stress was operationalized by predicting strain at time 3 from stress at time 2 after removing the effects of stress at time 3. The formula for this ordered regression analysis is: strain at time 3 = (1) controls on strain at time 2 and on Pay Grade and Education, (2) stress E_s at time 3, (3) stress E_s at time 2, (4) Wife social support at time 3, (5) Wife social support at time 2, (Predictors (4) through (5) are discussed in Chapter V.)

Question 3 asks whether an increase in stress from time 2 to time 3, i.e., (stress time 3 - stress time 2) > 0, is positively related to high strain at time 3 over and above strain time 2. Because stress at time 2 is preceded by a minus sign in the change score we expect the partial correlation between stress at time 2 and strain at time 3 to be negative. [The regression formula relating change in strain to change in stress is: w_a strain $time_3$ - w_b strain time 2 = w_c stress time3 - w_d Stress time2. Or, adding w_b strain time2 to both sides of the equation, W_a strain time3 = w_b strain time2 + w_c stress time3 - W_d stress time2 (where w's are all positive)]. The algebra accounts for a prediction that is seemingly contrary to our hypotheses regarding the stress-strain relationship, namely that prior stress will be negatively related to subsequent strain.

<u>Descriptive Findings</u>

Before attempting to test the hypotheses and to answer the research questions it will be useful to present some descriptive data on stress and strain. Table IV-1 provides means and variances of stress, social support and strain of the leavers and stayers at all data collection times for each group. The table also includes the results of student t tests contrasting the two groups of respondents at times one and three on the major variables in the study. In Chapter VI, similar analyses using product-moment correlations instead of t-tests will be presented (see Table VI-1).

The leavers had significantly different stress at time one than the stayers for four of the five measures - Job Complexity, Work Load, Role Ambiguity, and Underutilization of Abilities. Of the four stresses, the findings for the latter two measures indicate that the leavers experienced greater stress than the stayers. The data for the first two stresses show that the leavers had less Job Complexity and less Work Load than the stayers. As will be argued below, we conclude that low values on these variables for the leavers are associated with higher stress, not lower

Table IV-1

Means and variances, for leavers and stayers at times one, two and three on stress, social support and strain. Also included are results of student t tests comparing the two groups of respondents at times one and three.

Variable	Leavers		Stayers			
	Mean	Variance	Mean	Variance	t value	Significance level
Time One:						
Job Complexity, E_s	5.64	1.08	6.06	.73	-5.64	$<$ .001
Work Load, E_s	3.56	.67	3.74	.41	-2.89	$<$ .004
Role Ambiguity, E_s	1.43	.99	1.21	.73	2.86	$<$ .005
Underutilization of Abilities, E_s	1.68	1.41	1.36	1.18	3.55	$<$ .001
Marital Stress, E_s	3.53	.43	3.46	.37	1.49	N.S.
Social Support, Wife, E_s	3.68	.97	3.62	.86	.88	N.S.
Social Support, Supervisor, E_s	2.99	.78	3.34	.42	-5.40	$<$ .001
Social Support, Coworkers, E_s	3.22	.32	3.26	.24	-.78	N.S.
Marital Dissatisfaction	1.55	.83	1.32	.84	3.21	$<$ .002
Anxiety	1.84	.47	1.41	.14	8.88	$<$ .001
Depression	1.56	.33	1.40	.16	3.76	$<$ .001
Irritation	1.61	.43	1.73	.25	-2.40	$<$ .02
Somatic Complaints	1.23	.071	1.19	.043	1.69	N.S.
Job Dissatisfaction	2.53	6.05	1.97	4.93	2.99	$<$ .003
Education	2.90	.82	2.98	.70	-1.13	N.S.
Pay Grade	7.13	.86	7.74	.84	-8.43	$<$ .001

<u>Time Two:</u>						
Job Complexity, E_s	5.32	1.53				
Work Load, E_s	3.33	.50				
Role Ambiguity, E_s	1.12	1.00				
Underutilization of						
Abilities, E_s	1.83	1.65				
Marital Stress, E_s	3.52	.46				
Social Support, Wife, E_s	3.67	.85				
Social Support, Supervisor, E_s	3.39	.49				
Marital Dissatisfaction	1.28	.86				
Anxiety	1.62	.24				
Depression	1.67	.27				
Irritation	1.59	.30				
Somatic Complaints	1.25	.083				
Low Self-esteem	1.50	1.30				
Job Dissatisfaction	1.60	4.17				
<u>Time Three:</u>						
Job Complexity, E_s	5.25	1.26	5.79	.74	-5.43	<.001
Work Load, E_s	3.30	.48	3.64	.38	-5.47	<.001
Role Ambiguity, E_s	1.09	.80	1.23	.76	-1.76	N.S.
Underutilization of						
Abilities, E_s	1.84	1.43	1.21	.89	5.96	<.001
Marital Stress, E_s	3.45	.46	3.49	.39	-.62	N.S.
Social Support, Wife, E_s	3.66	.75	3.60	.67	.71	N.S.
Social Support, Supervisor, E_s	2.99	.73	3.16	.57	-2.11	< .05
Marital Dissatisfaction	1.27	.74	1.41	.77	-1.74	N.S.
Anxiety	1.43	.26	1.43	.19	.04	N.S.
Depression	1.45	.28	1.44	.19	.22	N.S.
Irritation	1.62	.29	1.69	.29	-1.49	N.S.
Somatic Complaints	1.22	.073	1.21	.051	.29	N.S.
Low Self-esteem	1.56	1.37	1.28	1.09	2.67	< .01
Job Dissatisfaction	1.70	4.50	1.85	4.37	-.77	N.S.

stress, as is the case with the stayers. The leavers had lower Social Support from their supervisors than the stayers at time one did, with no differences between the groups on wife or co-worker support. The leavers, at time one, also had higher values on four of seven strains - Marital Dissatisfaction, Anxiety, Depression, and Job Dissatisfaction-with the stayers having higher Irritation at that time. The stayers also had higher Pay Grade than the leavers, prior to the latter leaving the Navy.

At time three, the leavers still had greater values than the stayers on Underutilization of Abilities. As occurred at time one, the leavers had lower values on Job Complexity and Work Load than the stayers. Also, the stayers reported more supervisory Social Support than the leavers. The leavers and stayers differed on only one strain: the leavers had lower Self Esteem than the stayers.

In addition to considering how stress, social support and strain differed between the groups at each time we were also interested in how the values changed within each group over time. We performed t-tests contrasting means at two adjacent time points for each respondent group separately. The types of stress, social support, and strain for these analyses are the same as those listed in Table IV-1. For leavers, the t-tests compared means at time 1 with those at time 2, and means at time 2 with those at time 3. For stayers, the means at time 1 were compared with those at time 3. Table IV-2 presents the results of the three sets of t-tests.

The leavers showed a significant change in three of the five E_s stresses from time 1 to time 2. Job Complexity, Workload, and Role Ambiguity all decreased during the interval. From time 2 to time 3 only one stress showed a change; Marital Stress declined significantly. Supervisor Support, but not Wife Support, increased, but only from time 1 to time 2 when the men changed from a Navy supervisor to a civilian supervisor.

The changes in strains for the leavers present a mixed picture. The strains of Marital Dissatisfaction, Anxiety, and Job Dissatisfaction decreased from time 1 to time 2 and Anxiety, Depression and Somatic Complaints declined from time 2 to time 3. These drops in strain are consistent with the notion that adjustment to the major life event of a career change occurs very quickly after the actual moves have transpired. The temporary increase in Depression could be an indication of a reaction to the losses experienced by separation from the Navy, whereas the decline

Table IV-2
Changes in stresses and strains. Pairwise t-tests[1] comparing values at two points in time for different respondents.

Variables	Leavers t_1 to t_2	Leavers t_2 to t_3	Stayers t_1 to t_3
Job Complexity	3.42***	1.32	3.25**
Work Load	1.09***	-.21	.48
Role Ambiguity	5.98***	-.61	-.52
Underutilization of Abilities	-1.68	.08	.91
Marital Stress	-.70	2.65**	-.11
Social Support, Wife, E_s	.75	1.19	1.46
Social Support, Supervisor, E_s	-3.66***	—	2.68**
Marital Dissatisfaction	8.53***	-1.66	-4.42***
Anxiety	7.22***	7.83***	-.47
Depression	-4.15***	9.15***	-1.04
Irritation	.76	-1.23	.65
Somatic Complaints	-1.57	2.68**	-1.03
Low Self-esteem	-5.81***	-1.40	-.22
Job Dissatisfaction	5.66***	.05	-.86

***$p < .001$
**$p < .01$
*$p < .05$

[1] Negative t-value indicates an <u>increase</u>, from the earlier to the later time period.

in Self-esteem suggests that the men had not fully become comfortable with their new work and family roles.

In sum, the leavers showed several changes in their levels of stress, social support and strain over the seven months of data collection. As measured by E_s, three stresses, Job Complexity, Work Load, and Role Ambiguity showed decreasing values over time. Supervisor Social Support, but not Wife Social Support, improved over time. By time 3, all of the strains had diminished except Low Self-esteem, which had still not shown any improvement. These findings indicate that the major adjustment to the midlife career change of our retiring Navy enlisted men had occurred within six months of Navy separation.

The stayers, who were not experiencing a major life change, showed considerably fewer changes in stress, social support, and strain. Job complexity E_s decreased and the two other changes listed in Table IV-2 were for the worse - the stayers' Supervisor Support diminished, and their Marital Dissatisfaction increased. We have no satisfactory explanation for these changes.

The stayers have been described as a comparison group for the leavers. Strictly speaking, however, they do not qualify as a control group because the data from them were collected approximately five months later, on the average, than that from the leavers. Hence, the two groups could have been affected by different seasonal or historical factors or events. Nonetheless, the data in Table IV-2 indicate that the leavers showed many (13 of 27) significant changes over time that were consistent with their status as a group undergoing a life change whereas the stayers showed substantially fewer (3 of 14) changes as a group.

After leaving the Navy, a portion of the leavers enrolled in training schools or college rather than seeking employment. At time 2, 135 men were exclusively students whereas 276 men worked at least part time. At time 3, the totals for students and workers were 45 and 401, respectively. We checked to see if these two groups differed on the major variables in the study or according to relationships between major variables, e.g., stress-strain. There were no systematic or large differences between students and workers so the two groups were combined for the analyses which follow in this report.

Results

The main method used to test the hypotheses discussed in Chapters IV and V involved ordered, multiple regressions. In three instances, the same regression analyses provided results relevant to the topics of both chapters - stress in Chapter IV and social support in Chapter V. The order of predictors in the regressions was stress, followed by social support, and then by an interaction term, stress x social support. Results regarding the main effects of stress are reported in Chapter IV whereas results regarding the main effects of social support are reported in Chapter V. The interaction term yields results pertaining to stress buffering by social support, a topic also dealt with in Chapter V. Specific instances in which the same regressions provided data for tables in Chapter IV and in Chapter V are as follows: Table IV-3 and Table V-2; Table IV-4 and Table V-3; Table IV-9 and Table V-4. Also, Table V-6 presents buffering findings which were part of regressions that provided results for Table IV-4 and Table V-3. All of the regression analyses in Chapters IV and V controlled for education and paygrade.

(1) Hypothesis la: Stress increases strains.

a. Cross-sectional tests of the main effects of stress on strain.

Ordered, multiple regressions with strain as the dependent variable and stress E_s (at the same time) as the first predictor were performed to test the hypothesis. Table IV-3 presents the findings. For both the leavers and the stayers the significant main effects of stress are produced primarily by Role Ambiguity and Underutilization of Abilities - the greater the stress, the greater the strain. The findings for Job Complexity and Workload of the stayers are primarily insignificant. For the leavers, of the 21 correlations over the three times between Job Complexity and strain and between Work Load and strain, 9 and 4, respectively, are significant in the negative direction. These results were unexpected because earlier research in our program (Caplan, et al., 1980) showed positive relations between these measures and strain. It may be that, for the leavers, work environments with low job complexity and low work load are stressful because the situations are not challenging and hence are unfulfilling and lead to strain (Bowers, 1975). This explanation proposes that low E_s is stressful for the leavers and it highlights the need for P_s measures to disentangle the seemingly contradictory findings. The relation between fit measures of Job Complexity and strain should clarify this issue (see

Table IV-3.
The main effects of stress E_s on strains. After controls on education and pay grade, the order of predictors in the cross-sectional multiple regressions was: stress E_s, social support (Wife E_s), stress x social support. Cell entries are the partial correlations between stress and strain without controlling on the subsequent predictors.

Stress	Marital Dissatisfaction	Anxiety	Depression	Irritation	Somatic Complaints	Low Self-esteem	Job Dissatisfaction
Stayers at Time 1							
Job Complexity							
Work Load				.14*			
Role Ambiguity						.18**	
Underutilization of Abilities	.20**		.17*			.18**	.24***
Marital Stress							
Stayers at Time 3							
Job Complexity							-.19*
Work Load							
Role Ambiguity		.26**	.20*	.23**		.20*	
Underutilization of Abilities	.17*	.18*	.19*	.20*		.18*	.34***
Marital Stress							
Leavers at Time 1							
Job Complexity	-.12**						-.10**
Work Load							-.09*
Role Ambiguity		.08*	.21***	.19***	.09*	.08*	.22**
Underutilization of Abilities	.10**	.10*	.14***	.12**		.12**	.37***
Marital Stress							

Table IV-3 (Cont'd.)
Subjects are Leavers (workers + students)

Stress	Marital Dissatisfaction	Anxiety	Depression	Irritation	Somatic Complaints	Low Self-esteem	Job Dissatisfaction
Leavers at Time 2							
Job Complexity	-.11*					-.14**	-.27***
Work Load						-.11*	-.18***
Role Ambiguity		.19***	.13**	.21***	.20***		.32***
Under utilization of Abilities						.17***	.45***
Marital Stress					.09*		
Leavers at Time 3							
Job Complexity	-.13**		-.13**			-.11*	-.25***
Work Load							-.21***
Role Ambiguity	.18***	.13***	.21***	.20***		.16***	.41***
Underutilization of Abilities	.16***	.18***	.27***	.17***	.10*	.27***	.48***
Marital Stress	-.11*		-.10*				

*$p < .05$
**$p < .01$
***$p < .001$

results for Hypotheses 2a and 2b in this chapter and for the decision to leave in Chapter VI).

Marital Stress did not produce any systematic relationship with strain for either group. Table III-6 also indicates that this measure had the lowest coefficient alpha of the stresses (=.49). Hence, Marital Stress may not be a good measure of stress. Alternatively, a fit measure may be necessary for this variable (see below).

b. Longitudinal tests of the main effects of stress on strains.

Ordered, multiple regressions with strain at time 3 as the dependent variable and stress E_s at time 2 as the first predictor provide data relevant to the hypothesis. Table IV-4 presents the findings. The results for Role Ambiguity and Underutilization of Abilities provide strong support for the hypothesis. The findings for Job Complexity and Workload again indicate that low values of these variables are related to strain.. Except for the relationship between Workload and Marital Dissatisfaction all of the entries in Table IV-4 are replicated in Table IV-3 for the leavers at time 2 and/or time 3. The order of magnitude of the correlations in the different instances are similar except that Job Dissatisfaction shows a greater relationship to stress in cross-sectional tests than in longitudinal tests.

The cross-lagged correlations were also examined, paying due attention to the pitfalls in the method (Rogosa, 1980). The data provide no additional information about Hypothesis 1a because the difference between the two sets of lagged correlations was too strongly influenced by the differences in the standard deviations of the stresses and strains to make any comparisons meaningful.

In sum, the data support Hypothesis 1a. Stress is related to strain cross-sectionally and stress produces strain over time.

(2) Hypothesis 1b: Moving one's residence during retirement will increase strain.

Zero-order correlations between the number of changes in residence during the career change and strains at times 2 and 3 were calculated. Table IV-5 presents the relevant data. Only one of the fourteen correlations is significant and in the predicted direction; the others show similar weak trends. Hence, the hypothesis receives very weak, if any, support.

Table IV-4. A longitudinal test of the effects of stress on strain. In ordered multiple regression analyses, strains at t_3 were predicted from: (1) stresses at time 2, (2) social support (Wife E_s) at time 2, (3) the product of stress at time 2 x social support at time 2. Education and pay grade were controlled. the cell entries are the partial correlations of stress at time 2 with strains at time 3. The subjects are leavers.

Stress at time 2	Marital Dissatisfaction	Anxiety	Depression	Irritation	Somatic Complaints	Low Self-esteem	Job Dissatisfaction
Job Complexity	-.13*						
Work Load	-.12*					-.14*	-.12*
Role Ambiguity		+.18**	+.16**				+.18**
Under-utilization of Abilities						+.15**	+.23**
Marital Stress					+.10*		

*p <.05
***p< .01

Table IV-5. Zero-order correlations between the number of changes in residence (i.e. zero, one, two) during the six months following Navy separation and strains at time two and at time three. Subjects are leavers.

Strains	Time two N=465[1]	Time three N=450
Marital Dissatisfaction	.01	-.01
Anxiety	.07	.02
Depression	.08	.07
Irritation	.07	-.01
Somatic Complaints	-.01	-.01
Low Self-esteem	.07	.01
Job Dissatisfaction	.002	.11*

*$p < .05$

[1] At time two, the frequency of changes, i.e. zero, one, two, were 166, 260, 39 respectively.

(3) Hypothesis 1c: The lower the transferability of job skills, the greater the strain.

The test for this hypothesis involved zero-order correlations between transferability of job skills and strains, all at time 3. The data in Table IV-6 indicate that all of the correlations are in the predicted direction. The two significant correlations show that the stress of low transferability of job skills is related to Job Dissatisfaction and Low Self-esteem, two strains most relevant to the job situation. Hence, the data support Hypothesis 1c.

Hypothesis 2a: Misfit between the person and his environment will explain additional variance in strain, over and above the additive effects of E_s and P_s.

A series of stepwise multiple regressions were performed to determine how much additional variance in strains was accounted for by the three fit measures of Poor Fit, Deficiency Fit, or Excess Fit. Each stepwise analysis began by constraining the E and P components of a P-E fit variable to be the initial predictors of a strain in a multiple regression equation. Following this, if one of the fit measures on the P-E fit variable accounted for a significant amount of additional variance in strain it was added to the equation. Good Fit is not included in this analysis because it is an additive combination of E_s and P_s and, hence, could not account for any additional variance.

There is a linear dependency amongst the three fit measures of "Poor Fit," "Deficiency Fit," and "Excess Fit" (Conway and Klem, personal communication). Thus, each of the three measures accounts for an equal amount of additional variance in strain. The results of the regression analyses show, therefore, whether or not a fit measure of stress accounts for additional variance in strain, without indicating any one specific measure of fit.

Table IV-7 presents the results relevant to Hypothesis 2a. The entries in the first column of each time give the percent of variance in strain accounted for by the additive effects of environmental demands received (E_s) and desired (P_s). The second column gives the additional percent of variance accounted for by the fit measure of stress.

For each P-E fit variable, there are 21 opportunities in Table IV-7 for a fit measure to account for additional variance over and above E_s + P_s. Hypothesis 2a is strongly supported by the results. Both Job

Table IV-6

Zero-order correlations between perceived transferability of job skills at time three and strains at time three. Subjects are leavers.

Strains	Correlations N = 430
Marital Dissatisfaction	-.06
Anxiety	-.03
Depression	-.09
Irritation	-.07
Somatic Complaints	-.07
Low Self-esteem	-.17*
Job Dissatisfaction	-.27*

*$p < .01$

Table IV-7.

Additional variance in strains accounted for by measures of fit with respect to stress (Poor Fit, Deficiency Fit, Excess Fit). The samples used were leavers at time 1, time 2, and time 3. The entries in the first column (E+P) give the percent of variance accounted for by the additive effects of the amount of environmental demands received (E) and the amount of demands desired (P). The entries in the second column give the additional percent of variance accounted for by a fit measure of stress with significant ($p < .05$) predictive power.

Stress = Job Complexity

	Time 1		Time 2		Time 3	
Strains	E + P	Fit	E + P	Fit	E + P	Fit
Marital Dissatisfaction	.013		.016		.020	
Anxiety	.001	.009	.009		.017	
Depression	.013	.007	.014	.010	.014	
Irritation	.018	.012	.007		.013	
Somatic Complaints	.005		.003		.002	
Low Self-esteem	.004	.010	.020		.028	
Job Dissatisfaction	.031	.031	.093	.016	.072	.023

Table IV-7 (Cont'd.)

Stress = Role Ambiguity

Strains	Time 1		Time 2		Time 3	
	E + P	Fit	E + P	Fit	E + P	Fit
Marital Dissatisfaction	.017		.016	.013	.035	.025
Anxiety	.020		.051	.017	.014	
Depression	.046		.021	.020	.043	.021
Irritation	.043	.012	.070		.039	.012
Somatic Complaints	.009		.053		.008	
Low Self-esteem	.016		.011		.024	
Job Dissatisfaction	.047	.012	.121		.159	

Stress = Marital Stress

Strains	Time 1		Time 2		Time 3	
	E + P	Fit	E + P	Fit	E + P	Fit
Marital Dissatisfaction	.112	.035	.130	.079	.143	.029
Anxiety	.004		.013	.024	.030	.031
Depression	.017	.011	.015	.033	.040	.037
Irritation	.005		.015	.028	.028	.035
Somatic Complaints	.001		.030	.033	.026	.019
Low Self-esteem	.027	.006	.053	.017	.051	.041
Job Dissatisfaction	.001		.019		.021	

Complexity and Role Ambiguity had eight such significant instances. Marital stress produced 15 instances in which a fit measure accounted for significant additional variance.

The amounts of additional variance accounted for by the fit measures were: 0.7% to 3.1% for Job Complexity, 1.2% to 2.5% for Role Ambiguity, and .06% to 7.9% for Marital Stress.

(4) Hypothesis 2b: The worse the fit between the person and his environment, the greater the strain.

Question 1: Are there meaningful patterns in the relationships that different forms of misfit have with strain?

To evaluate Hypothesis 2b and Question 1, ordered cross-sectional multiple regressions with strain as the dependent variable and stress F_s as the first predictor were performed. Four sets of regressions were performed at time 1 and at time 3 for the leavers; one set for each of the four types of fit discussed in Chapter III - Good Fit, Poor Fit, Deficiency Fit, Excess Fit.

Table IV-8 presents the relevant data. In general, the findings strongly support the hypothesis - 85 of 168 possible entries (7 strains x 3 stresses x 4 fit measures x 2 times) are significant in the predicted direction.

For Job Complexity, the four forms of misfit are about equally predictive of strain with poor fit having a slight edge over deficiency fit, excess fit, and good fit. Also, the fit measures of Job Complexity had almost the same proportion of significant correlations with strain, 19 of 56, as did the E_s measures of Job Complexity in Table IV-3, 6 of 14 (for time 1 plus time 3). This substantiates Hypothesis 2B that fit measures for Job Complexity would be predictive of strain, just as Es measures are predictive of strain (Hypothesis 1A).

For Role Ambiguity, all four forms of misfit produced significant correlations with strain at Time 1 whereas all but deficiency fit did so at time 3. The fit measures yielded a smaller proportion of significant relationships with strain, 38 of 56, than did the stress E_s measure of Role Ambiguity in Table IV-3, 12 of 14. A comparison of the different fit measures indicates that Excess Fit is most predictive of strain at both times. Hence, an excess of role ambiguity in the work setting over what is desired is related to more strain than a deficiency of role ambiguity.

Table IV-8 The main effects of stress F_s on strains. After controls on education and pay grade, the order of predictors in the cross-sectional multiple regressions was: stress F_s, social support (wife E_s), stress x social support. Fit measures of stress are: good fit (GF), poor fit (PF), deficiency fit (DF), excess fit (EF). Cell entries[1] are the partial correlations between stress and strain without controlling on subsequent predictors. Positive correlations are predicted in every instance. Subjects are leavers at time one and time three.

Stress, Time 1	Marital Dissatisfaction	Anxiety	Depression	Irritation	Somatic Complaints	Low Self-esteem	Job Dissatisfaction
Job Complexity, GF			.09*	.13***			
Job Complexity, PF		.08*	.13***	.14***		.11**	.24***
Job Complexity, DF	.11*					.08*	.12**
Job Complexity, EF			.13***	.16***			.17***
Role Ambiguity, GF	.13***	.15***	.18***	.19***	.09*	.13***	.17**
Role Ambiguity, PF			.10*	.16***			.18***
Role Ambiguity, DF	.11**	.12**	.11**	.08*		.11**	
Role Ambiguity, EF	.12**	.13***	.19***	.24***	.10**	.11**	.22***
Marital Stress, GF	.27***		.10*			.14***	
Marital Stress, PF	.18***		.10*				
Marital Stress, DF	-.11**						
Marital Stress, EF	.35***	.09*	.15***	.08*		.16***	

Table IV-8 (Cont'd.)

Stress, Time 3	Marital Dissatisfaction	Anxiety	Depression	Irritation	Somatic Complaints	Low Self-esteem	Job Dissatisfaction
Job Complexity, GF							-.15**
Job Complexity, PF	.14**						.21***
Job Complexity, DF							.14**
Job Complexity, EF	.10*						.12*
Role Ambiguity, GF	.13**	.10*	.18***	.18***	.11*	.13**	.27***
Role Ambiguity, PF	.15**			.16***			.13*
Role Ambiguity, DF							
Role Ambiguity, EF	.18***	.11*	.18***	.16***	.10*		.14**
Marital Stress, GF	.23***	.13**	.11*	.12**	.11*	.20***	
Marital Stress, PF	.11*	.15**	.17***	.16***	.11*	.16***	
Marital Stress, DF							
Marital Stress, EF	.26***	.17***	.13**	.13**	.14**	.15**	

***$p < .001$
**$p < .01$
*$p < .05$

With Marital Stress, practically all of the significant, positive relationships with strain at both time 1 and time 3 involve either Good Fit, Excess Fit, or Poor Fit. Thus, a discrepancy between home tasks the wife is seen to demand and home tasks the man desires to do leads to strain, especially when there is an excess of demands over desires. These findings stand in sharp contrast to the lack of significant results for Marital Stress E_s, i.e., the perceived demands of the wife, and strain. This is the best example in our data of the superiority of fit measures of stress rather than traditional E_s stress measures for explaining resultant strain.

In conclusion, both Table IV-7 and Table IV-8 present data that confirm predictions of Person-Environment Fit Theory. Fit measures account for significant variance in strain over and above that due to what is desired and obtained per se. Measures of stress which consider what the person desires from the environment as well as what the person obtains from the environment are also predictive of strain.

Question 2: Do the current data replicate earlier findings of French, et al., 1982: a). Job Complexity - Poor Fit and Underutilization of Abilities decrease Job Dissatisfaction, b). Underutilization also increases Irritation?

The relevant entries in Table IV-8 demonstrate that, for both times 1 and 3, the predicted positive relationships between Job Complexity - Poor Fit and Job Dissatisfaction are highly significant and among the strongest in the entire table. Table IV-3 indicates that the positive relationship between Underutilization of Abilities and Job Dissatisfaction is the strongest relationship between stress and strain at each time for each group of subjects. The correlation between Underutilization of Abilities and Irritation was significant for 2 of 3 times for the leavers and for 1 of 2 times for the stayers. In sum, the current data provide very good replication of earlier findings in our research program about the effects of specific stresses upon specific strains. This replication is important because the earlier study controlled on up to 57 variables and cross-validated the findings four times. It is unlikely, then, that the present findings could be an artifact of confounding.

Hypothesis 3: Environmental stress has greater effects upon more relevant dependent strains than upon less relevant strains.

Our measures of stress focus upon two domains: home and work. Our strains contain dissatisfaction measures that separately pertain to each domain, a self-esteem measure probably more relevant to work than to home, and three affective strains and one ill health strain equally relevant to both domains. The relevance hypothesis predicts that environmental stress will have a greater effect upon strains relevant to the same domain rather than to a different domain. For example, the job stress of Underutilization of Abilities should have a greater effect upon the job strain of Job Dissatisfaction than upon the home strain of Marital Dissatisfaction (see also French, et al., 1982).

Table IV-3 shows that, for the stayers, there is no support for the relevance hypothesis at time 1, and some support at time 3 - the relation between Underutilization of Abilities and Job Dissatisfaction being the highest of all stress-strain pairs. One difficulty here is that the one measure of home stress, Marital Stress, is not related significantly to any strain.

For the leavers, Table IV-3 indicates that the highest correlations at each time are typically between work stresses E_s and Job Dissatisfaction which supports the relevance hypothesis. Similarly, although the correlations at time 3 between the work stresses and the home strain of Marital Dissatisfaction are also sometimes positive and are relatively high, they are smaller than the correlations between the work stresses and Job Dissatisfaction. Thus, the relevance hypothesis receives support in the data for the leavers using stress E_s measures.

Table IV-8 contains correlations between stress F_s and strain that pertain to the relevance hypothesis. For Job Complexity at Times 1 and 3, the strongest relationships are with Job Dissatisfaction, in support of the hypothesis. Role Ambiguity shows conflicting results - at Time 1 higher correlations with Job than Marital Dissatisfaction but, at Time 3, higher correlations with Marital than Job Dissatisfaction. Marital Stress is most highly correlated with the home strain of Marital Dissatisfaction at Time 1 but this is equivocal at Time 3.

In sum, the observed relations between stress and strain give support to the relevance hypothesis within the work domain. On the other hand, for the home domain, there is no support for the relevance hypothesis using stress E_s measures and only minimal support with stress F_s measures. Many stress E_s and F_s measures are strongly related to the general strains, however.

Question 3: Regarding the distinction between the effects of acute stress from those of chronic stress - will the rate of increase in stress account for additional variance in subsequent strain beyond that accounted for by the final level of stress?

The question was addressed using a multiple regression analysis with strain at time 3 as the dependent variable. The control variables were strain at time 2, education, and pay grade. The order of predictors pertinent to Question 3 were stress E_s at time 3, and then stress E_s at time 2. Table IV-9 provides the relevant data.

As mentioned above, the two stress E_s measures of Role Ambiguity and Underutilization of Abilities provided the strongest support, relative to the three remaining stress E_s measures (Job Complexity, Workload, Marital Stress), for Hypothesis IA: The greater the stress, the greater the strain. Hence, it would be best to consider Question 3 using the stresses of role ambiguity and underutilization of abilities.

Table IV-9 indicates that stress E_s (Role Ambiguity and Underutilization of Abilities) at time 3 is significantly related to an increase in strain from time 2 to time 3 in 13 of 14 cases. This result taken alone, is ambiguous. It may reflect the effect of chronic, unvarying stress or it may reflect the effect of a change in stress or acute stress. To resolve this issue, it is necessary to examine the relation between stress E_s at time 2 after having controlled for stress E_s at time 3; i.e., to evaluate the effect of a change in stress from time 2 to time 3. The relevant data in Table IV-9 must be considered in light of the point made at the initial mention of Question 3 earlier in the chapter; namely, that because of the algebra the relation between stress at time 2 (controlling on stress at time 3) and strain at time 3 (controlling on strain at time 2) should be negative. Table IV-9 shows that for Role Ambiguity and Underutilization of Abilities, an increase in stress is significantly related to an increase in strain in 7 of 14 cases, and all 7 cases show the predicted negative relation. Hence, Question 3 receives an affirmative answer in our data for the stresses of Underutilization of Abilities and Role Ambiguity. When this finding is added to the earlier results for Hypothesis la, we have strong support that stress is related to strain cross-sectionally and that acute change in stress produces a significant increase in strain over time.

Table IV-9.

A longitudinal test of the hypothesis that a change in stress produces a change in strain. Dependent variable was strain at time 3. After controlling for strain at time 2, pay grade, and education, the order of predictors on the multiple regressions was: stress (E_s) at time 3, stress (E_s) at time 2, social support (E_s) at time 3, social support (E_s) at time 2, the product of stress at time 3 x social support at time 3, the product of stress at time 2 x social support at time 2. The cell entries are the partial correlations of each stress at time 2 or 3 with strains at time 3, controlling on preceding (in the regression model), but not subsequent, predictors. Subjects are leavers.

Stress	Marital Dissatisfaction		Anxiety		Depression		Irritation		Somatic Complaints		Low Self-esteem		Job Dissatisfaction	
	t_3	t_2	t_3	t_2	t_3	t_2	t_3	t_2	t_3	t_2	t_3	t_2	t_3	t_2
Job Complexity													-.16**	.14*
Work Load		-.12*											-.19***	
Role Ambiguity	.17**	-.11*	.14*		.24***		.21***		.12*	-.12*	.19***		.37***	-.12*
Underutilization of Abilities	.15**		.14*		.19***	-.16**	.12*	-.11*		-.17**	.18**		.37**	-.23**
Marital Stress					-.11*	.11*								

***p < .001; **p < .01; *p < .05

CHAPTER V

SOCIAL SUPPORT

In this chapter we shall be replicating many of the findings from our previous cross-sectional studies of the beneficial effects of social support on stress and strain. These findings will be extended by testing the hypotheses longitudinally, by utilizing fit measures of social support, and especially by exploring further the possibility that negative buffering as well as positive buffering exists (see LaRocco, et al., 1980). The more detailed hypotheses and research questions will be discussed before the results are presented.

Hypotheses and Research Questions.

Hypothesis 1: Social support from other people reduces environmental stresses at work and in the home.

Hypothesis 2: Social support reduces strains.

Hypothesis 2 refers to the level of the independent variable, social support, and it is an appropriate formulation for studying stable levels of social support. However, it has been reported that sudden losses of social support (i.e., loss events) and sudden increases in social support (gain events) will have effects on strain over and above the effects of the final level of social support. We may formulate this quantitatively as Question 1: Will the magnitude of increase or decrease in social support produce decreases or increases respectively in strain when we hold constant the final level of social support?

In this formulation of Question 1, both the independent and the dependent variables are change scores over the same time interval. Therefore, the independent variable is not antecedent to the dependent variable, and any interpretation of the direction of causation is equivocal. For this reason among others we have investigated Question 1 by multiple regression analyses which substitute for change in strain the prediction of strain at time 2 after controlling for strain at time 1. The change in social support is operationalized by predicting strain at time 2 from antecedent social support at time 1 after first removing the effects of contemporary social support at time 2. For predicting strain at time 2 the order of predictors in this ordered multiple regression is: Strain at time 2 = (1) controls on strain at time 1 and on Education and Pay Grade, (2) E_s stress at time 2, (3) E_s stress at time 1, (4) Wife social support at time 2, (5) Wife social support at time 1, (6) E_s stress at time 2 x wife social support at time 2, (7) E_s stress at time 1 x wife social support at time 1. Only the results from steps (4) and (5) are reported in this chapter. Although this analysis does separate the effects of prior support from the effects of contemporary support, the effects of change in support are not clearly separable.

Hypothesis 3: Person-environment fit with respect to social support will explain additional variance in strain over and above the additive effects of its components, i.e., environmental social support (E_s) and desired social support (P_s).

Hypothesis 4: The more relevant the dependent stresses and strains are to social support the greater will be the effects of social support on these dependent variables. An independent and a dependent variable will be more relevant if both belong to the same domain: marital dissatisfaction is more relevant to social support from one's wife (same domain) than it is to social support from one's supervisor (different domain). Similarly job dissatisfaction is more relevant to support from one's supervisor than it is to support from one's wife. Most of our strains do not refer clearly to one domain or another. For example, the negative affects - anxiety, depression, irritation - make no reference to job or home. Among these, however, depression is the most relevant to social support because it contains a large element of loneliness and lack of friendly interaction while social support provides friendly interaction and the supplies which lonely people lack.

Hypothesis 5: Social support will act as a buffer to reduce the effect of stress on strain. This is the meaning of "the buffering hypothesis" in most previous research (see for example, Caplan et al., 1975; Cobb, 1976; House, 1981; LaRocco et al., 1980; French et al., 1982). These interaction effects were predicted to be beneficial; and if opposite results were sometimes obtained they were discarded as chance occurrences (Pinneau, 1975). However, LaRocco et al. (1980), found that when stress was measured as person-environment misfit, F_s, (but not when measured as E_s) social support from the supervisor (but not from other sources) increased the effects of stress on strain. This opposite effect to the usual buffering they labelled negative buffering. Graphs depicting examples of positive and negative buffering are shown in Figure V-1. Not much was said about negative buffering because it was unexpected and because it was not certain that the occurrence exceeded chance. Accordingly, we made additional analyses in the same data set of 28 instances of positive and negative buffering of F_s measures of stress. These were broken down by three sources of social support, and the ratio of positive to negative buffering was tabulated for each source. These ratios were: 1/10 for the supervisor, 8/1 for co-workers, and 8/0 for people at home. These results indicate clearly that negative buffering is not a random occurrence, and they suggest that our analyses in this chapter should distinguish between different sources of support and between the two types of measures of stress.

Descriptive Findings

We have noted above that our measures of subjective social support probably reflect to some degree objective support. Some indication of this relation is available only in the case of support from the wife. We have asked the man how much support he receives from his wife and we have asked his wife, using the same questions, how much support she provides for her husband. The wife's report can be taken as an objective measure in the sense that it is independent of the husband's report, but we assume that it also reflects her biases just as the measure of subjective social support reflects his biases. The actual correlation between these objective and subjective measures of social support is .34. In view of this modest correlation we should avoid assuming that objective and subjective social support are the same thing.

A comparison of the mean levels of social support received by leavers vs. by stayers at time 1 and again six months later shows some interesting results (see Table IV-1). There is no difference between leavers and stayers in support from their wives, either at time one or six months later. However, the leavers compared to the stayers report significantly less social support from their supervisors at both times. The biggest difference occurs at time 1 when both groups are reporting about their Navy supervisors ($p<.001$ by t-test). This difference may well be one factor in

Figure V-1. Typical examples of positive and negative buffering of social support (from different sources, as indicated) on relationships of stress to strain. (Dashed vertical lines represent actual distribution limits for stress and strain variables expressed in standard scores.)

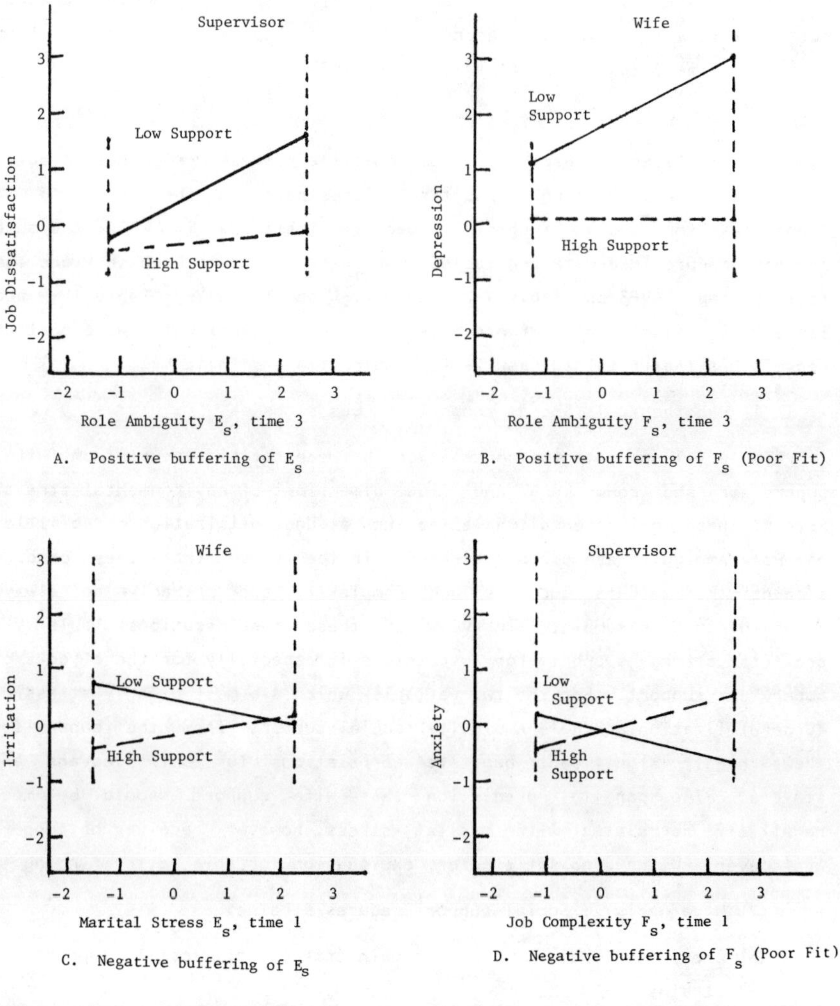

the decision to retire, a possibility that will be explored in more detail in Chapter VI.

There are no significant changes over time in support from the wife, but there is a large increase among leavers in supervisory support from time 1 to time 2 ($p<.001$ by t-test, Table IV-2).

Results

As indicated in Chapter IV, some multiple regressions generated data, part of which are reported in Chapter IV for stress, and the remaining in Chapter V for social support. Specific instances in which the same regressions provided data for tables in Chapter IV and in Chapter V are as follows: Table IV-3 and Table V-2; Table IV-4 and Table V-3; Table IV-9 and Table V-4. Also, Table V-6 presents buffering findings which were part of regressions that provided results for Table IV-4 and Table V-3.

(1) Hypothesis 1: Social support reduces stresses.

Table V-1 presents the correlations between social support from wife, supervisor and co-workers and five dimensions of environmental stress. Some of these environmental variables such as Underutilization of Abilities and Role Ambiguity are clearly stressful in the sense that they produce strains; but others such as Job Complexity are probably not always stressful in this sample. In view of these considerations Table V-1 presents strong support for Hypothesis 1, especially for the effects of supervisor support. For the two variables which are most clearly stressful (Underutilization and Role Ambiguity) social support from the supervisor shows highly significant negative correlations for both leavers and stayers. The parallel prediction that wife support should be most negatively correlated with marital stress, however, receives no support whatsoever. We have no satisfactory explanation for this latter finding.

(2) Hypothesis 2: Social support reduces strains.

(a) Cross-sectional tests of the main effects of social support on strains.

The basic findings for this analysis are presented in Table V-2. The overall results provide highly significant and consistent support for the hypothesis that social support reduces strains. Each of the seven strains is reduced by social support in at least three of the five groups.

Social support by the wife (E_s) and social support by the wife (Deficiency Fit) have similar effects, but the former tends to have

Table V-I. Zero order correlations between social support E_s and stress E_s at time 1.

Leavers

Stress E_s	Wife E_s (N=680)	Supervisor E_s (N=680)	CoWorker E_s (N=260)
	Social Support		
Job Complexity	.15***	.08*	.08
Work Load	.07	-.04	.07
Role Ambiguity	-.07	-.35***	-.30***
Underutilization of Abilities	-.11**	-.23***	-.15*
Marital Stress	.04	-.02	.05

Stayers

Stress E_s	Wife E_s (N=215)	Supervisor E_s (N=215)	CoWorker E_s (N=215)
	Social Support		
Job Complexity	.02	.13	.04
Work Load	.09	-.06	-.08
Role ambiguity	-.10	-.23***	-.16*
Underutilization of Abilities	-.29***	-.32***	-.07*
Marital Stress	.12	.10	-.01

*** $p < .001$
** $p < .01$
* $p < .05$

Table V-2. The main effects of social support by wife and by supervisor on strains. After controls on education and pay grade, the order of predictors in the cross-sectional multiple regressions were: stress (E_s), social support, stress x social support. Cell entries are the range, across five stresses, of the partial correlations between social support and strain controlling on the preceeding predictors.

Source of Social Support	Marital Dissatisfaction	Anxiety	Depression	Irritation	Somatic Complaints	Low Self-esteem	Job Dissatisfaction
Stayers at Time 1							
Wife E_s	-.69** to -.71**	-.20* to -.22*	N.S. (-.05 to -.10)			-.38** to -.42**	
Wife Def.	-.61** to -.65**	-.26** to -.28**	N.S. (-.09 to -.13)	N.S. -.12 to -.15^{+}		-.35** to -.38**	
Sup. E_s	N.S. -.13 to -.19**	-.26** to -.31**	-.28** to -.32**	-.32** to -.36**		-.14 to -.20	-.20* to -.27**
Stayers at Time 3							
Wife E_s	-.71** to -.72**	-.18^{+} to -.20^{+}				-.40** to -.42**	
Wife Def.	-.46** to -.49**	N.S. -.14 to -.22*		N.S. -.10 to -.17^{+}		-.28** to -.34**	
Sup. E_s		-.20^{+} to -.26*	-.32** to -.35**	-.49** to -.51**			-.23* to -.27**
Leavers at Time 1							
Wife E_s	-.61** to -.62**	-.10* to -.12*	-.26** to -.27**	-.17** to -.19**		-.37** to -.38**	N.S. -.06 to -.08^{+}
Wife Def.	-.57** to -.58**	-.15** to -.16**	-.23** to -.25**	-.18** to -.19**		-.30** to -.32**	
Sup. E_s	N.S. -.06 to -.08^{+}	-.10^{+} to -.12*	N.S. -.05 to -.14**	-.08^{+} to -.14**	N.S. -.07 to -.10*	N.S. -.04 to -.08^{+}	-.10^{+} to -.17**
Leavers at Time 2							
Wife E_s	-.68**	-.15* to -.18**	-.30** to -.32**	-.29** to -.32**	-.12* to -.15*	-.33** to -.36**	-.19** to -.23**
Wife Def.	-.57** to -.60**	-.19** to -.21**	-.22** to -.23**	-.26** to -.28**	-.15** to -.23**	-.21** to -.24**	-.12* to -.15*
Sup. E_s				-.19^{+} to -.25*	N.S. -.09 to -.19^{+}		-.30** to -.44**

Table V-2 (Cont'd.)

Source of Social Support	Marital Dissatisfaction	Anxiety	Depression	Irritation	Somatic Complaints	Low Self-esteem	Job Dissatisfaction
Leavers at Time 3							
Wife E_s	-.69** to -.71**	-.18** to -.22**	-.33** to -.36**	-.24** to -.27**	N.S. -.08 to -.14*	-.26** to -.30**	N.S. -.05 to -.14*
Wife Def.	-.51** to -.55**	-.14* to -.24**	-.22** to -.32**	-.16** to -.23**	-.13* to -.17**	-.17** to -.25**	N.S. -.05 to -.14*
Sup. E_s	N.S. -.10 to -.18+	-.25** to -.30**	-.19* to -.28**	-.24** to -.29**	N.S. -.14 to -.18*	N.S. -.10 to -.21*	-.38** to -.49**

+$p < .05$; *$p < .01$; **$p < .001$.

stronger effects on Marital Dissatisfaction and on Low Self-esteem. This does not contradict Hypothesis 3 which asserts that fit measures will account for <u>additional</u> variance even though their effects may be weaker (see below).

In Table V-2 there are no meaningful differences between time 1 and time 3 for stayers who were not experiencing any general life changes. For leavers, on the other hand, who were experiencing considerable life change at time 2 there is a consistent, but very slight, tendency for wife support to have stronger effects on strain at time 2. Probably supervisory support has its weakest effects at time 2 because some of the men were in school instead of in a job, and they answered the questions on social support in reference to their teachers. The rest of the men had new supervisors whose support was generally less effective than at either time 1 or time 3. By time 3 wife support has stronger effects on Depression and Irritation for leavers than for stayers.

(b) Longitudinal tests of the main effects of social support on strains.

The lagged effects of social support were examined because it is possible to interpret the above cross-sectional findings in the reversed direction, for example to assume that depression causes low subjective social support. This interpretation becomes less plausible when the social support <u>precedes</u> the depression. However, the lagged effects of social support would be expected only when the causal interval is appropriate. A first step in the analysis showed that for wife support (both E_s and Deficiency Fit) the short interval from time 1 to time 2 showed no more effects than the longer interval from time 2 to time 3. Accordingly, Table V-3 presents the results for the latter interval where it is more appropriate to test for the effects of supervisory support.

Table V-3 shows strong effects of prior social support on subsequent strains, and the magnitudes of these lagged partial correlations are only slightly smaller than the corresponding cross-sectional correlations in Table V-2. This additional support for Hypothesis 2 should be interpreted cautiously, however, because of the substantial correlation between social support at time 2 and social support at time 3 (r=.76 for Wife Support). The cross-lagged correlations were also examined, paying due attention to the pitfalls in this method (Rogosa, 1980). The results provided no further information about Hypothesis 2 because the difference between the

Table V-3. A longitudinal test of the effects of social support on strain. In ordered multiple regression analyses, strains at t_3 were predicted from: (1) stresses at time 2, (2) social support at time 2, (3) the product of stress at time 2 x social support at time 2. Education and Pay Grade were controlled. The cell entries are the range, across five stresses, of the partial correlations of social support at time 2 with strains at time 3. The subjects are leavers.

Social Support at time 2	Marital Dissatisfaction	Anxiety	Depression	Irritation	Somatic Complaints	Low Self-esteem	Job Dissatisfaction
Wife E_s	-.46** to -.53**	N.S. -.08 to -.11*	-.15** to -.19**	-.16** to -.17**		-.20** to -.21**	-.14** to -.15**
Wife Def.	-.50** to -.53**	-.17** to -.18**	-.25** to -.26**	-.20** to -.21**	-.15** to -.16**	-.20** to -.23**	-.13** to -.15**
Sup. E_s	-.16* to -.21*		-.20** to -.24**				-.34** to -.41**

**$p < .01$

*$p < .05$

two lagged correlations was so strongly influenced by the differences in the standard deviations.

Research Question 1 concerning the effects of change in the level of social support was investigated by means of ordered multiple regression analyses. The formula predicts that the coefficients for contemporary social support (step (4) in the equation) should be negative, indicating that contemporary social support reduces strains just as it does in the cross-sectional analyses reported in Table V-2. However, prior social support (step (5) in the equation) is expected to show positive coefficients if an increase in social support from time 2 to time 3 reduces strain. The reason for this apparent reversal is due to the fact that an increase in social support is given by a positive value of (SS_3-SS_2), which involves a negative term for social support at time 2.

The results pertinent to Question 1 are presented in Table V-4. Before discussing these results we note that the contemporary effects of social support from the wife (wife Es3) are negatively related to each of the strains except Somatic Complaints and Job Dissatisfaction where the trends are in the predicted direction but not significant. This merely confirms the results in Table V-3.

As predicted, the results for prior social support at time 2 (wife Es2) are always positively related to strain, when they are significant. However, these significant results occur for only two strains. The greater the increase in social support E_s, by the wife, the greater the decrease in Marital Dissatisfaction; but the Deficiency measure of social support shows only a weak trend in the same direction. Similarly the E_s measure of wife support, but not the Deficiency measure of wife support, is significantly related to depression. Again the greater the increase in support the greater the decrease in depression. So the answer to Question 1 is a qualified "yes"; a change in social support will produce a corresponding change in some, but not all, strains which is over and above the strain attributable to the final level of social support. Further research is needed to clearly separate the effects of change in social support from the effects of the prior level of social support.

(3) Hypothesis 3: Person-environment fit (F_s) with respect to social support will explain additional variance in strain beyond the additive effects of its components, E_s and P_s.

Table V-4. The relation of change in social support to change in strain. Longitudinal ordered multiple regression analyses were used to predict strains at time 3 from prior and from contemporary stress and social support. The order of predictors was: 1) controls on pay grade, education and strain at time 2, 2) stress at time 3, 3) stress at time 2, 4) social support at time 3, 5) social support at time 2, 6) stress x social support at time 3. Only the results for steps 4) and 5) are reported here. The measures of social support are Wife E_s and Wife Deficiency Fit at times 2 and 3. The subjects are leavers.

Social Support	Marital Dissatisfaction	Anxiety	Depression	Irritation	Somatic Complaints	Low Self-esteem	Job Dissatisfaction
Wife E_{s3}	-.45** to -.48**	N.S. -.11 to -.15**	-.28** to -.36**	-.16** to -.23**		N.S. -.10 to -.17**	
Wife E_{s2}	.14+ to .18**		.12+ to .18**	N.S. .08 to .11+	N.S. .08 to .13*	N.S. .08 to .11+	
Wife DF_3	-.29** to -.32**	N.S. -.09 to -.13*	-.22** to -.27**	N.S. -.10 to -.11+	N.S. -.09 to -.12+	N.S. -.08 to -.16**	N.S. -.03 to -.12+
Wife DF_2	N.S. .05 to .12+						

$^{**}p < .001$; $^{*}p < .01$; $^{+}p < .05$

This hypothesis was tested in a series of ordered multiple regression analyses in which the effects of E_s and P_s on strains were first removed and then it was determined if a PE fit measure of social support accounted for additional variance. The results in Table V-5 show that PE Fit accounted for significant additional variance in all strains except low self esteem and job dissatisfaction.

Although the results for PE Fit on social support are highly significant (9 out of 21 cells are significant at the 5 percent level), the amount of additional variance explained is small, varying from .8 percent to 4.8 percent. In other studies, only fit with respect to stresses has been examined. In this study such fit with respect to stresses accounted for from 1% to 8% of additional variance (see Chapter IV). Similarly, House reports a range of 1.2% to 2.7% in a community sample (House, 1972); and a study of stresses in high school students found that PE fit measures of stress accounted for from 1% to 5% additional variance (Kulka, 1976). The largest amount of additional explained variance (1.5% to 14%) has been reported by French, et al., 1982. In that study the use of PE fit measures typically doubled the total explained variance in strain.

We should note here that a fit measure with respect to social support from the wife has its strongest effects on the most relevant dependent variable, namely Marital Dissatisfaction. It has no effects on the least relevant variable - Job Dissatisfaction. We may conclude that misfit with respect to social support from the wife, especially after leaving the Navy, has a substantial effect on strains. The magnitudes of the partial correlations between Deficiency Fit and Marital Dissatisfaction, pertaining to the first row of Table V-5, were .31 at time two and .20 at time three.

(4) Hypothesis 4: The more relevant the dependent variable is to the independent variable the stronger the effect.

We have noted above that Table V-5 provides some support for this hypothesis. Even stronger support is evident in Table V-3: Wife support has partial correlations with the most relevant strain, Marital Dissatisfaction, ranging from -.46 to -.53 and with the least relevant strain, Job Dissatisfaction, ranging from -.13 to -.15. In contrast, supervisory support correlates only -.16 to -.21 with Marital Satisfaction, now the least relevant strain, whereas it correlates -.34 to -.41 with the most relevant strain - Job Dissatisfaction.

Table V-5. Additional variance in strains accounted for by measures of fit with respect to social support by the wife (Poor Fit, Deficiency Fit, Excess Fit). The samples used were leavers at time 1, time 2, and time 3. The entries in the first column (E + P) give the percent of variance accounted for by the additive effects of the amount of wife support received (E) and the amount of wife support desired (P). The entries in the second column give the additional percent of variance accounted for by a fit measure of social support with significant ($p < .05$) predictive power.

	Time 1		Time 2		Time 3	
Strains	E + P	Fit	E + P	Fit	E + P	Fit
Marital Dissatisfaction	.410	.008	.488	.048	.509	.020
Anxiety	.024		.042	.015	.066	.009
Depression	.074		.121		.145	.010
Irritation	.039		.113	.010	.075	
Somatic Complaints	.009		.018	.010	.024	.008
Low Self-esteem	.152		.125		.092	
Job Dissatisfaction	.008		.049		.020	

Even stronger support for the relevance hypothesis is evident in the cross-sectional analyses of the effects of stress on strain. Table V-2 shows that Wife social support F_s typically correlates close to -.70 with the most relevant strain (Marital Dissatisfaction) and typically has little or no significant correlation with the least relevant strain (Job Dissatisfaction). Similarly supervisory support always correlates significantly with Job Dissatisfaction with r's ranging from -.10 to -.49, but it is often unrelated to Marital Dissatisfaction (the highest such correlation is -.19).

When the dependent variable is stress (E_s) the results are more mixed (see Table V-1). Supervisors and co-workers are both in the work domain, so their support should reduce work stresses but have less effect on marital stress. This is true for Role Ambiguity but not for Job Complexity and Work Load. Wife support, on the other hand, should have strongest effects in reducing marital stress and weaker effects on job stresses. The results are just the opposite: wife support has no significant effects on Marital Dissatisfaction, but it does reduce Underutilization of Abilities and perhaps Job Complexity. Since these are cross-sectional correlations, the direction of causation could be reversed: men who are utilizing their best abilities in a complex job may receive more social support from their wives.

(5) Hypothesis 5: Social support will act as a buffer to reduce the effects of stress on strain. In this section we discuss first the evidence for cross-sectional buffering of environmental stress (E_s), then the longitudinal test for this same buffering, and finally the cross-sectional buffering of fit measures of stress (F_s) compared to E_s measures of stress.

The cross-sectional buffering of stress E_s by social support was tested in 105 ordered multiple regressions (7 strains x 5 stresses x 3 measures of social support) in each of 5 groups (stayers at times 1 and 3 and leavers at times 1, 2, and 3). The basic tables for these interaction effects (i.e., buffering) are presented in Appendix E. An examination of these tables shows that all stresses, all strains, all measures of social support and all groups are involved in some instances of buffering but there is no simple patterning of these results. Furthermore, there is very little replication of specific findings from one group to another and from one time to another. For example, among stayers at time 3 the strongest partial correlation is -.24 for the positive buffering of Somatic

Complaints by Supervisor Support; but this is not replicated in any of the other four groups.

Since we found no replicated and meaningful specific patterns, we summarize the results in Appendix E in terms of a clear general pattern revealed by the ratio of positive to negative instances of buffering. Summing across all five groups, the main finding is that positive buffering is more frequent than negative buffering. The grand totals show a ratio of 55 instances of positive buffering to 26 instances of negative buffering. There are similar ratios for each of the three measures of social support (22/7 for Wife Support E_s, 14/10 for Wife Support Deficiency Fit, and 19/9 for Supervisor Support E_s). With so large a number of cells we would expect by chance that 52.5 would be significant at the 10% level if these were independent events, but we know that all of the variables tend to be intercorrelated so the expected number is higher than 52.5. The obtained number of significant instances of buffering (55+26=81) may not be significantly greater than chance, but it is certain that the pattern of these ratios is not a chance distribution.

The longitudinal test of this same buffering hypothesis consists of longitudinal multiple regressions predicting to strains at time 3 from stress and social support at time 2. Table V-6 presents the partial correlations for the interactions of stress at time 2 multiplied by social support at time 2. The number of significant interactions, indicating buffering, is 10 out of 105 possible, which is at the chance level. The pattern of the findings also seems random, with four of the 10 significant interactions indicating positive buffering. So these findings do not replicate the predominance of positive over negative buffering which was found in the cross-sectional analysis. A similar analysis of longitudinal buffering of E_s stress x wife social support over the shorter time interval from time 1 to time 2 gave similar results. Seventeen percent of the tests were significant at the 10% level; and the pattern seemed random except that the ratio of positive to negative buffering was 9/1, which is more similar to the cross-sectional results.

We turn now to the buffering of stress as measured by PE fit, F_s. The multiple regressions for leavers at times 1 and 3 (not reported here) can be summarized simply. Each table has about twice the expected number of significant instances of buffering but the partial correlations are low, scattered, and do not replicate well from time 1 to time 3. However, one pattern stands out: the buffering is predominantly negative. The ratios of

Table V-6.

Longitudinal buffering in leavers from time 2 to time 3. In ordered multiple regressions, strains at time 3 were predicted from: (1) stresses at time 2, (2) social support at time 2, (3) the product of stress at time 2 x social support at time 2. Education and Pay Grade were controlled. The cell entries are the partial correlations for step (3), the product of stress x social support (either Wife Support E_s or Wife Deficiency Support or Supervisor Support E_s). A negative correlation indicates positive buffering.

	Marital Dissatisfaction			Anxiety			Depression			Irritation			Somatic Complaints			Low Self-esteem			Job Dissatisfaction		
	Wi E_s	Wi Def.	Sup E_s	Wi E_s	Wi Def.	Sup E_s	Wi E_s	Wi Def.	Sup E_s	Wi E_s	Wi Def.	Sup E_s	Wi E_s	Wi Def.	Sup E_s	Wi E_s	Wi Def.	Sup E_s	Wi E_s	Wi Def.	Sup E_s
Job Complexity																		-.13*		+.13**	
Work Load																-.09*					
Role Ambiguity					-.12**		+.09*														
Underutilization of Abilities		+.14**	+.20**																-.11**		
Marital Stress		+.10**																			+.26***

***$p < .01$
**$p < .05$
*$p < .10$

positive to negative buffering are 10/19 for the supervisor and 8/12 for the wife. This contrasts with the positive buffering of E_s, shown in Appendix E, where the overall ratio was 55/26.

The above overall summaries of the buffering hypothesis give a general picture which is difficult to interpret for several reasons. First, the predictions of buffering of two stresses, Job Complexity E_s and Work Load E_s, are equivocal because these "stresses" did not generally produce strains in the analyses reported in Chapter IV. Perhaps we should predict negative buffering for these strains. However, as expected the fit measures of these two stresses showed clear positive correlations with strains. Second, the data for leavers at time 2 are suspect because some of these men had no job supervisor and none of the others had known their new civilian supervisors long enough for one to expect strong buffering. Accordingly, our next analysis of buffering was limited to those groups and times where we could most precisely compare buffering of E_s with buffering of F_s measures of stress. Table V-7 shows how buffering differs as a function of the source of support (Wife vs. Supervisor), Stress E_s vs. Stress F_s and stayers vs. leavers.

The most striking findings in Table V-7 pertain to the differences between wife support and supervisor support. When support is buffering stresses measured by E_s, both sources show a predominance of positive buffering over negative buffering with the ratio for the wife (19/6) being slightly more positive than for the supervisor (13/8). When the measure of stress is Poor Fit ($|E-P|$) these ratios shift dramatically to 6/0 for the wife vs. 1/10 for the supervisor. Adding these together, the totals for F_s (7/10) are predominantly negative buffering while the comparable ratios for E_s are mainly positive (16/10). Finally, we note in Table V-7 that the stayers have relatively more positive buffering (16/4) than the leavers (16/10). These latter findings are opposite to Cobb's predictions (1976) that evidence for positive buffering will be found more often in periods of change and readjustment to stress than in periods of stable chronic stress.

The actual curves for positive and for negative buffering which are derived from our multiple regression analyses might show various forms. In order to examine whether they conformed to theoretical expectations, we plotted the curves for all the significant cases of buffering for leavers at times 1 and 3 (except for 11 significant interactions involving Job Complexity and Work Load). The resulting 32 graphs showed essentially two types: (1) all of the 15 cases of positive buffering were much like those

Table V-7. Cross-sectional buffering of Stress E_s and of Stress F_s (Poor Fit) by social support E_s from the wife and from the supervisor. Subjects are Stayers at times 1 and 3 and Leavers at times 1 and 3. Entries are the ratios of significant cases of positive to negative buffering.

	Social Support Wife E_s X Stress E_s	Social Support Supervisor E_s X Stress E_s	
Stayers Time 1	4/0	3/1	16/4
Stayers Time 3	7/2	2/1	
Leavers Time 1	2/4	3/1	16/10
Leavers Time 3	6/0	5/5	
	19/6	13/8	

	Social Support Wife E_s X Stress F_s (Poor Fit)	Social Support Supervisor E_s X Stress F_s (Poor Fit)	
Leavers Time 1	2/0	1/7	7/10
Leavers Time 3	4/0	0/3	
	6/0	1/10	

reported in the literature (see the top two examples in Figure V-1); (2) all of the 17 cases of negative buffering showed the lines for low social support intersecting the lines for high social support (see the bottom two examples in Figure V-1). The high social support line showed a positive slope (strain increases with increasing stress), but the low social support line showed a surprising negative slope (strain decreases with increasing stress).

In these multiple regression equations which yielded negative buffering, an examination of the coefficients showed that all cases except two showed the expected negative coefficient for social support, i.e., the main effect of social support was to reduce strain. However, the expected main effect of stress in increasing strain was absent except in one instance. To summarize, negative buffering occurs where: (1) there are the predicted main effects of social support (decreasing strain); (2) there is an absence of the predicted main effects of stress (increasing strain); (3) the absence of a main effect of stress on strain is because the slope of the stress-strain curve is positive under high social support but negative under low social support so that the opposing effects on strain cancel each other.

In order to understand negative buffering and the conditions which produce it we need first to explain the negative slope of the stress-strain curve under low social support. When the measure of stress is Poor Fit, this negative slope occurs exclusively when the supervisor is the source of support and never when the wife is the source of support. When the measure of stress is E_s, the negative slope of the stress-strain line is more often produced by the supervisor but it does occur twice when the wife is the source of social support. In 12 of the 17 cases of negative buffering by the supervisor the strain which is affected is one of the clinical strains (Anxiety, Depression, Irritation or Somatic Complaints) which contrasts with a previous finding that negative buffering by the supervisor occurred only for job-related strains (LaRocco et al., 1980).

The explanation of why there is a negative slope for the stress-strain curve when supervisory support is low must be quite speculative at this time. However, three possibilities can be mentioned. First, it may depend on difference in the behavior of the unsupportive supervisor when stress is high vs. low. At high levels of stress he makes allowances for the difficulty of the job and does not blame the man for poor performance but at low levels of stress he blames the man for low ability or poor motivation. The man reacts with more depression, irritation or anxiety under high blame than under low blame. Second, the negative slope may be more specifically related to the kind of job stress. For example, low role ambiguity may produce more strain than high ambiguity because the non-supportive supervisor is using close supervision which restricts the man's freedom of action and he is held accountable by clear and unavoidable role demands, so he feels more threatened. The wife and the supportive supervisor avoid both of these behaviors; they do not blame the man for low or poor motivation and they do not use threatening close supervision. Instead, they provide emotional support which generally prevents anxiety, depression and irritation. The third possible explanation of the negative stress-strain slope stems from the observation of differences in buffering depending on whether the stress is measured by E_s or F_s.

Since the buffering of fit measures of stress (F_s) are predominantly negative buffering whereas the buffering of one component (E_s) is generally positive, we concluded that this difference may be due to the effects of the other component (P_s). Accordingly we examined next the interactive effects of P_s and social support on strains as well as the main effects of P_s on strains. First, we note that the main effects of P_s on strains have been reported in Tables III-4, III-5, III-6 and III-7 of Caplan, et al., 1980. In these tables the P_s measures refer to what the respondent would like his job to be or what he prefers in a job. In each table this desired or preferred characteristic of the job refers to a different dimension: job complexity, responsibility for persons, role ambiguity, and quantitative work load respectively. In twelve instances the P_s measure is significantly related to strains, and in every one of these instances the relation is inverse - high P_s is related to low strain. The most plausible interpretation of this cross-sectional relation is to assume that low strain causes high levels of aspiration with respect to desired goals, and conversely high strain (and the correlated high stress) causes the men to adapt by lowering their goals for the kind of job they would like to have.

In this study of Navy men we had similar measures of desired (i.e., P_s) job complexity, role ambiguity and marital stress. Table V-8 presents both the main effects and the interactions with social support from the wife, the supervisor, and co-workers. As in Caplan et al., 1980, all of the 25 significant main effects are negative: low desired job characteristics are associated with high strain. Again the most reasonable

Table V-8. The cross-sectional main effects and interaction effects of P_s (i.e. goals) on strains at time 1. The order of the predictors in the ordered multiple regressions were: (1) controls on Education and Paygrade, (2) P_s at time 1, (3) social support at time 1, (4) P_s x social support at time 1. The cell entries are partial correlations for leavers at time 1.

Strains	Marital Dissatisfaction			Anxiety			Depression			Irritation			Somatic Complaints			Low Self-esteem			Job Dissatisfaction		
Social Support E_s	Wi	Sup	Co-W	Wi	Sup	Co-W	Wi	Sup	Co-W	Wi	Sup	Co-W	Wi	Sup	Co-W	Wi	Sup	Co-W	Wi	Sup	Co-W
Main Effects of P_s																					
Job Complexity P_s							-.10**	-.10**	-.12*	-.09*	-.09*								-.16**	-.16**	
Role Ambiguity P_s	-.11**	-.11**		-.12**	-.13**					-.08*	-.09*	-.16*				-.09*	-.08*				
Marital Stress P_s	-.37**	-.29**	-.35**				-.11**	-.12**	-.12*							-.14**	-.14**	-.21**			
Effects of P_s x Social Support																					
Job Complexity P_s							-.08*				-.08*										
Role Ambiguity P_s								-.06+													
Marital Stress P_s					-.07+			-.08*			-.07+							+.20**			

**p < .01
*p < .05
+p < .10

interpretation seems to be that the men adjust their goals and aspirations to the existing stresses and strains.

In Table V-8 the interactions between social support and desired job characteristics are significant at the 10% level about 10% of the time. However, five of the seven significant interactions are with supervisor social support and all five of these multiplicative terms (out of a possible 21) are inversely related to strains. An examination of the corresponding graphs for these five interactions shows that the general finding of a main effect of strain in reducing goals is reversed under a low supportive supervisor as contrasted to a highly supportive supervisor. Nothing can be said about the interactions with wife support and co-worker support because they are clearly not significant. Although these results on the interaction of P_s x social support may not be statistically significant, they are suggestive of interesting hypotheses for explaining the occurrence of positive and negative buffering. It is plausible that social influences on job goals will affect the influence of PE fit on strain. It is also plausible that the supervisor and the wife would often have opposing influences. And finally it is reasonable that these two sources of support will have the most opposite effects when reacting to person-environment fit and the affective strains of anxiety, depression and irritation.

CHAPTER VI

THE DECISION TO LEAVE: COMPARISON OF PERSONNEL LEAVING THE NAVY WITH THOSE WHO REENLISTED

In this chapter we turn our attention to the determinants of the decision to leave the Navy. It is obvious that from the Navy's point of view, retirement at a relatively early age (in our sample a mean of 39.5 years) represents undesirable attrition. High rates of attrition entail high costs and expenditure of scarce resources that need to be diverted to recruitment, selection and training of new personnel. Thus, excessive attrition may result in a Navy with less experience, lower efficiency and poorer performance. Understanding the factors that produce a high attrition rate can have many practical implications for manpower policy. This is obviously the case if, for example, some of the determinants of the decision to leave the Navy are affected by organizational practices that can readily be changed to produce better retention.

Early retirement is surely a significant contribution to manpower turnover in the Navy. The vast literature on employee turnover identifies several types of independent variables, predictors, or causes of job turnover (for reviews see Mobley et al., 1979; Porter & Steers, 1973; Price, 1977). The two broadest types are: (1) individual variables that include such subcategories as (a) demographic variables (e.g., age, education, and marital status) (b) job related individual variables (e.g., tenure, productivity), (c) personality and attitudinal variables (e.g., job satisfaction, organizational commitment), and (2) organizational variables (e.g., peer relationships, pay structure, leadership and job content). In their review of the literature on turnover, Mobley et al., (1979) concluded that "...age, tenure, overall satisfaction, job content, intentions to remain on the job, and commitment are consistently and negatively related to turnover" (p. 493). They also pointed out that generally, however, less than 20% of the variance in turnover is explained by these variables. Mobley and his associates urged researchers to develop clear conceptual models, in part by viewing turnover more broadly as a process that involves several types of variables.

Indeed, in recent years, researchers have already offered several elaborate conceptual models of the turnover process, and conducted a number of empirical tests (see, for example, Arnold & Feldman, 1982; Michaels & Spector, 1982). Both the conceptual and empirical work on these models have recently been reviewed and summarized by Bluedorn (1982a; 1982b). In this chapter we examine and extend the application of Fishbein and Ajzen's (1975) general model of attitudes and behavior to employee turnover. No attempt is made here to test this model since it has already been tested and used successfully in a number of investigations (Hom & Hulin, 1981; Newman, 1974). Instead, our aim is to provide evidence for the relevance of additional variables to the turnover process that are not considered explicitly by this, or other models. These variables provide information on important causes of the decision to stay on or leave one's job and organization. Most specifically we refer here to the role of job stress, strain, and social support as important substantive variables in the phenomenon of turnover.

Briefly stated, according to the Fishbein and Ajzen model, behavior is directly determined by behavioral intention which in turn is a function of the attitude toward the behavior and the subjective norm. While the attitude concept refers to a favorable or unfavorable affective evaluation of the behavior, the latter concept, subjective norm, refers to the belief that most significant others expect one to engage in the behavior. Each of these concepts can be measured directly at a global level or indirectly by assessing and assembling its components. In the case of attitude, it involves measuring the strength of various beliefs that certain outcomes will result from engaging in the behavior as well as the desirability, (i.e., valence or utility) of these outcomes. In the case of subjective norms, this measurement involved the assessment of the beliefs about the expectations of specific significant others and the motivation to comply with their expectations. Finally, according to the Fishbein and Ajzen's model, behavioral intention is the most direct proximal determinant of the behavior followed by the attitude toward the act and the subjective norms as the sole determinants of the intention. All other variables such as attitudes toward objects (e.g., Navy, Job), personality dispositions etc., influence behavior only indirectly, that is, through their effect on the attitude and the subjective norms.

Using an array of traditional predictive variables of turnover (e.g., job satisfaction, promotion, etc.) Hom and Hulin (1981) compared predictions of reenlistment in the Army National Guard made by two attitudinal models: the one proposed by Fishbein and Ajzen (1975) and the other by Triandis (1977). While reenlistment was strongly predicted by the two attitudinal models (R=.71 and .72) it was only moderately predicted by a multiple regression of job commitment and satisfaction and other traditional variables such as pay, promotions, and co-workers (R=.51).

There are a number of advantages for using attitudinal models for the prediction of job turnover. First, these models often include, and can easily accommodate, considerations and expectations with regard to alternative jobs, both at present and in the future. Indeed, the Mobley et al.'s (1979) review emphasized the importance of these considerations in the turnover process.

Second, Fishbein and Ajzen's attitude-behavior model, which is based on an expected utility approach (Mitchell & Biglan, 1971; Mitchell, 1974), has been proven useful in accounting for a great variety of volitional behaviors such as drinking (Schlegel et al., 1977), family planning (Davidson & Jaccard, 1979), drug use (Bentler & Speckart, 1979; 1981) and others (for reviews see Ajzen & Fishbein 1977; 1980). A somewhat earlier and similar version of this expected utility approach was also used successfully by Vroom (1964) to predict job performance.

Third, and perhaps most importantly, results from several recent studies using longitudinal designs and rigorous multivariate analysis techniques of model testing, such as LISREL (Joreskog & Sorbom, 1978), have conclusively demonstrated that attitudes do cause behavior (Bentler & Speckart, 1979; 1981; Kahle & Berman, 1979). It thus follows that the attitudinal variables incorporated in the models mentioned above not only predict or covary with behavior; they actually determine and explain it.

In most of the research using Fishbein and Ajzen's model, behavioral intention and attitudinal variables were shown to constitute the proximal determinants of volitional acts such as reenlistment or retirement. At the same time the question can be raised as to what are the distal determinants of the decision to stay on or to leave a job, that is, those factors that are involved in the formation of the attitudes themselves. Fishbein and Ajzen (1975) suggest that three categories of variables are involved as causes in the formation of attitudes toward acts. These are (1) personality variables, (2) attitudes toward objects (e.g., toward the Navy), and (3) demographic variables.

The present investigation suggests the importance of an additional category that includes environmental conditions. There is an abundance of evidence that job stress and social support from supervisor and co-workers influence health and perceived well being (Caplan et al., 1980; French et al., 1983; House, 1981; LaRocco et al., 1980). The findings show that stress defined as person-environment fit accounts for variance in strain over and above the variance accounted for by its component parts (French et al., 1982). These variables are thus hypothesized to be important determinants of the attitude toward staying on or leaving one's job. More specifically, stress and the resulting strain are hypothesized to produce a negative attitude toward the job, and consequently, a decision to leave. In contrast, social support on the job is hypothesized to produce a positive attitude and therefore is associated with a decision to stay on the job. Finally, and in line with the Fishbein and Ajzen's model, these variables are hypothesized to influence the decision to leave one's job or organization <u>indirectly</u>, that is, through their influence on the relevant attitudes toward staying or leaving the job or the organization, in our case, the Navy.

<u>Results</u>

In order to test the hypotheses regarding the role of stress, strain and social support in the formation of attitudes toward leaving the Navy the data were subjected to two types of statistical analyses. First, product moment correlations were computed between our independent variables in various categories and the decision to reenlist or retire, that is, to stay or to leave the Navy (coded 1 and 2, respectively). Second, a structural causal path model was constructed and statistical path analyses were performed. The model was based on the conceptual considerations regarding the direct and indirect influence of attitudinal, stress, strain, and social support variables on the decision to leave the Navy.

The significant product moment correlations between our various predictors and the decision to leave versus to reenlist are displayed in Table VI-1.

As can readily be seen, all of the attitudinal variables as reflected by relative valences of outcomes, were found to be moderately correlated with the decision to leave. An index that is based on the mean score of ten of the items, with a coefficient alpha of .84, is indeed the most highly correlated variable with the decision to leave the Navy (r=.39). In particular, those who decided to leave perceived civilian life to provide them with better opportunities than the Navy for (a) making friends at work, (b) developing new skills, (c) having the desired amount of responsibility at work, (d) gaining respect for their past Navy experience, (e) having a quality leadership supervisor, and (f) utilizing their major skills.

The subjective norm, as reflected by the measure of perceived family preference for leaving the Navy, was also significantly correlated with the decision to leave (r=.24).

Finally, it is important to note that several stress measures that were discussed in previous chapters (especially Chapter IV, Table IV-1) and social support from the supervisor were weakly but significantly correlated with the decision to leave the Navy. The greater the stress, and the lower the social support from the supervisor, the greater the tendency to leave. Similarly, the decision to leave is again correlated weakly but significantly with measures of strain such as dissatisfaction with the job, and the Navy. It also seems to be accompanied by anxiety depression and irritation.

Among the organizational factors, Pay Grade is negatively correlated with leaving; persons who are at the lower pay grades prefer leaving more than those who are at the higher pay grades. Although the correlation here is of moderate strength (r=-.27) it is among the highest correlates of the decision to leave. A possible reason for this relatively high correlation is that pay grade represents not only the level of pay but also the level of responsibility and utilization of abilities within the Navy.

The variables that did not have a statistically significant correlation with the decision to leave the Navy were Role Ambiguity, P, Work Load, E, and Social Support from Co-workers.

Next, we turn to the path analysis. Here a structural causal model was employed to trace the flow of influence from some variables to others and up to the decision to leave the Navy.

The statistical path analysis was performed twice: once for the early leavers (E) and stayers (S) subsample, and a second time for the leavers (L) and stayers (S) subsample. Separate analyses were required because each subsample of leavers included some unique variables not found in the

Table VI-1

Product Moment Correlations between Predictors and the Decision to Leave the Navy[1]

Measure	r	p	N
I. Attitudinal Variables			
Civilian vs. Navy Index[4]	.39	.001	374 ES[3]
Comparisons regarding items on:			
Friends at work	.32	.001	161 ES
Leisure time with family	.12	.02	374 ES
Rewards for job performance	.22	.001	374 ES
New skills, development	.27	.001	373 ES
Responsibility, having the desired amount	.31	.001	373 ES
Respect for past Navy experience	.28	.001	373 ES
Rules and discipline at the work place	.23	.001	373 ES
Job Security	.21	.001	372 ES
Leadership of supervisor	.26	.001	372 ES
Skill Utilization	.29	.001	375 ES
II. Subjective Norms			
Family preference for leaving vs. staying	.24	.001	902
III. Stress Measures and their Components			
Underutilization of Abilities	.12	.001	909
Job Simplicity[5], P	.10	.004	911
Job Simplicity, E	.18	.001	901
Job Simplicity, Excess Fit	.10	.002	900
Role Ambiguity, E	.09	.005	910
Work Load, P	.14	.003	477 LS[2]
IV. Social Support			
Supervisor Social Support on the job	-.18	.001	911
V. Strain Measures			
Navy Dissatisfaction	.16	.001	904
Job Dissatisfaction	.10	.003	905
Anxiety	.28	.001	908
Depression	.11	.001	907
Irritation	-.08	.02	908

Measure	r	p	N
VI. Organizational Factors and Others			
Paygrade	-.27	.001	912
Number of supervised personnel	-.10	.002	900
Age	-.16	.001	855

Note: 1. Decision to leave was assigned a high score; decision to stay, low score.
2. LS: Analysis is based on the combined data for the L subsample (L) of leavers and the stayers group (S).
3. ES: Analysis is based on the combined data for the E subsample (E) of leavers and the stayers group (S).
4. This index with a coefficient alpha of .84, included the sum of all the items mentioned below. A high score for the index and for the items reflects a more favorable attitude toward civilian job or life than toward the Navy.
5. The measures of Job Simplicity are the inverse of the corresponding measures of Job Complexity used in other chapters. I.e., Job Simplicity, P=1-Job Complexity, P, and so on for other E and fit measures.

other. In each case the analysis followed the following steps: First, all of our stress, strain, social support and organizational (e.g., pay grade) variables were correlated with the decision to leave the Navy. Second, those variables that were significantly correlated with the decision to leave (above the .05 level, see Table VI-1), were included as independent variables in a multiple regression analysis to predict the decision to leave. Several of the variables so specified, however, were left out. They included the affective strain measures of anxiety, depression and irritation and the single items that were included in the attitudinal index measure of civilian vs. Navy life. The exclusion of the affective measures was based on the ambiguity of their causal status; it is quite plausible that rather than causing the decision to leave, the affective strains constitute a consequence of that decision. The exclusion of the single items of the index measure was based on the fact that the index possessed a high coefficient alpha of .84 and was more highly correlated with the decision than any single item. The remaining variables that were found to have a statistically significant path (i.e., beta weight) beyond .05 level were included in our path diagrams.

Finally, because of the central role that the job satisfaction concept plays in nearly every investigation of job turnover, the path analysis also included the Navy and job dissatisfaction variables. Once included, multiple regressions were computed to account for these two variables. All of the previously mentioned stress and strain variables (excluding anxiety, depression and irritation) were used as independent variables. The additional stress and strain variables that were found to have a statistically significant path beyond the .05 level were again included in the final path diagrams. The results of these analyses are presented in Figures VI-1 and VI-2 for the two subsamples.

In each figure a structural causal model is displayed with the paths and their coefficients. The paths are represented by arrows, each begins with an independent variable (a cause) and points to a dependent variable (the effect or outcome). The path coefficients are estimated by the standardized regression coefficients, i.e., the beta weights. The paths displayed in the two figures were the only paths found in our analysis to be statistically significant at the .05 level.

The path model presented in Figure VI-1 provides some support for the view, presented earlier, that behavioral decisions are directly caused by the attitude toward the <u>alternative</u> courses of action as expressed by the relative valence of their outcomes which comprised our Civilian vs. Navy measure. It also suggests that the attitude is, in turn, caused by stress attributable to personal and environmental factors. More specifically, the decision to leave the Navy is directly determined by the <u>attitude</u> that the person has toward leaving for civilian life vs. staying with the Navy (path=.30). Only to a lesser extent is this decision affected directly by the family preference (path=.15), and by environmental or personal factors such as Pay Grade (path=-.10), Job Simplicity, E (path=.24) and by Excess of Job Simplicity (i.e., Job Complexity Deficiency Fit) (path=.14). Note that Job Simplicity is a measure of stress that leads to high strain; and therefore those who experience Job Simplicity and greater strain chose to leave the Navy. Furthermore, the attitude toward Civilian life vs. Navy, is shown according to this model to be determined by environmental and personal factors such as Job Ambiguity, E, Job Simplicity P, and dissatisfaction with the Navy.

As mentioned earlier, the data that were obtained from the subgroup of late leavers did not include the Civilian vs. Navy attitudinal measure. Consequently, the path model that is presented in Figure VI-2 does not contain this variable. Possibly for this reason the decision to leave the Navy here is shown to be determined directly by a greater number, and in greater part, by personal and environmental stress producing factors.

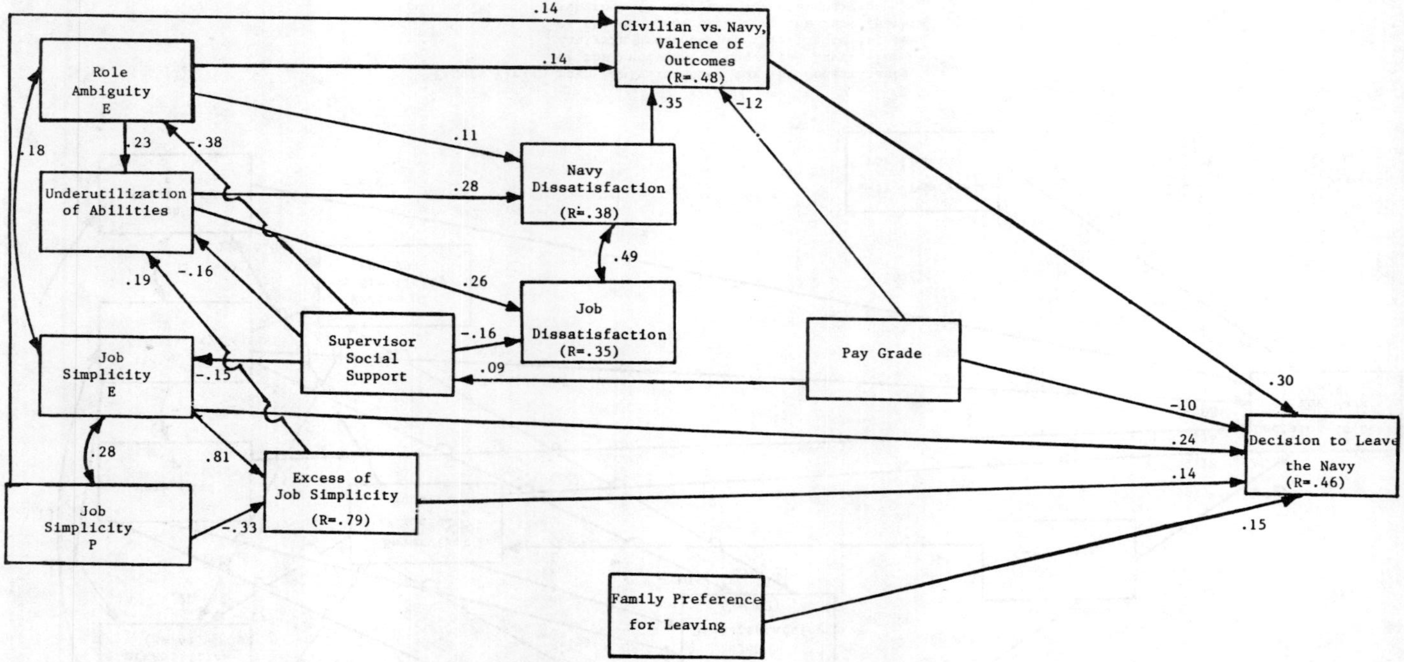

Figure VI-1: Path-Analysis Model for the Determinants of the Decision to Leave the Navy. The analysis presented in this figure is based on the combined data from the early leavers subgroup (N=260) and the stayers group (N=217).

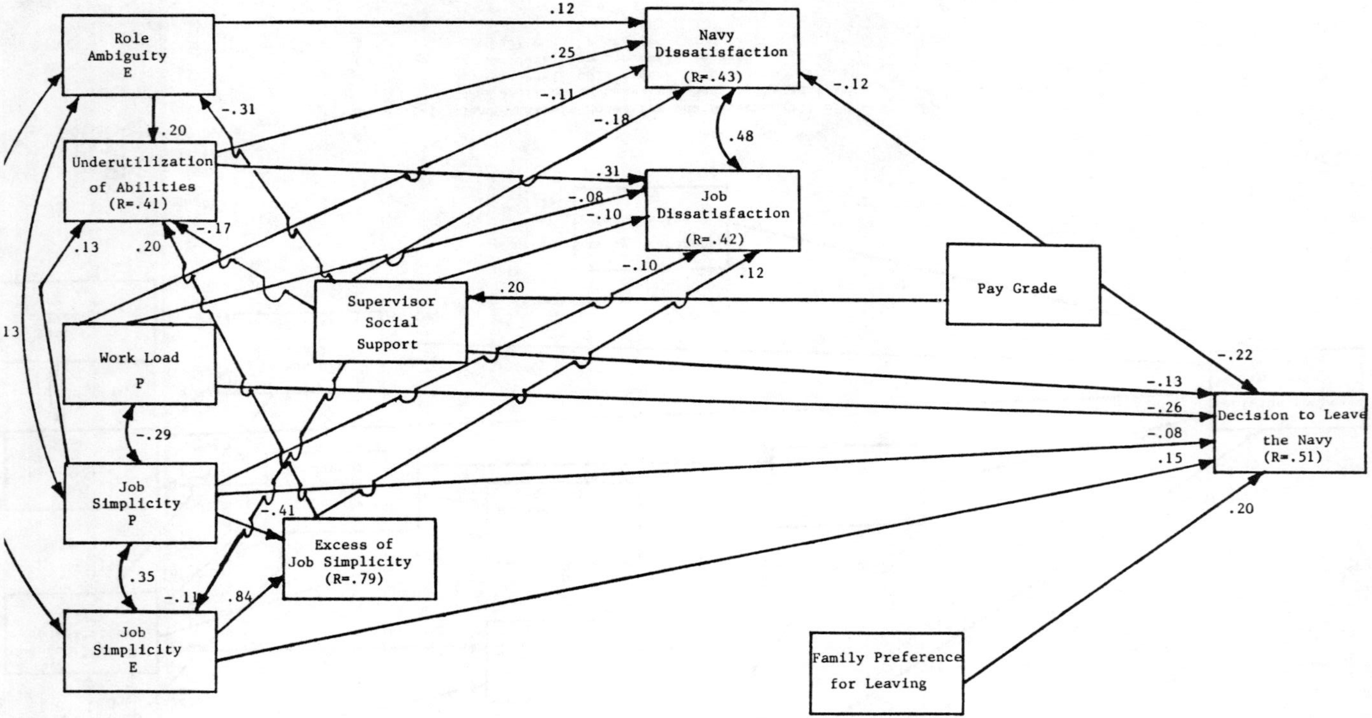

Figure VI-2: Path-Analysis Model for the Determinants of the Decision to Leave the Navy. The analysis presented in this figure is based on the combined data from the late leavers subgroup (N=435) and the stayers group (N=217).

Here, low social support from the supervisor, a preference for a lighter and more simple work load, low pay grade, too simple a job, and family preference for leaving contribute to the decision to leave the Navy rather than to stay in it.

Although the path models that are presented in the two figures are based on somewhat different subsamples and variables, they do exhibit important similarities. First, in both cases, dissatisfaction with the job or the Navy did not have a direct effect on the decision to leave. The model that included the subgroup of early leavers suggests that the dissatisfaction with the Navy has an indirect effect on the decision to leave, mediated by the attitudinal factor, i.e., the Civilian vs. Navy measure.

Second, in both cases, a person's pay grade is found to have a significant direct influence on the same three variables. Lower pay grade influences (1) the decision to leave rather than to stay in the Navy; (2) it also produces greater dissatisfaction with the Navy, but not with the job; and (3), it results in receiving less social support from the supervisor.

Third, in both cases, the family's preference for leaving vs. staying exerts a direct influence on the decision to leave.

Fourth, and perhaps most importantly, the social support provided by the supervisor has the same central role in the results exhibited by both models. It seems to have a relatively strong influence over a number of key stresses. High social support from the supervisor reduces the experience of being underutilized and the ambiguity about what is expected. It may also contribute to the assignment of jobs with greater complexity. In so doing, social support also reduces job dissatisfaction and Navy dissatisfaction both directly, and indirectly, through its influence on various stresses such as underutilization of abilities.

Discussion

The decision to leave the Navy was shown in our path analyses to be influenced by four major types of variables: attitudinal or valence (e.g., Civilian vs. Navy), organizational (i.e., Pay Grade), stress and strain (e.g., various components of our P-E fit model), social (supervisor) support and social (family) influence. Together, these variables predicted the decision to leave reasonably well with multiple correlations of .46 and .55 in our two subsamples.

The results of the path analysis, which were presented in Figure VI-1, were generally compatible with Fishbein and Ajzen's attitude-behavior model. They showed that the attitude toward the behavior as measured by our Civilian vs. Navy index is the main determinant of the decision to leave the Navy. This attitudinal variable accounts for almost half of the explained variance of the decision to leave. In addition, the subjective norm component of their model, which was represented by our measure of family preference, also has a significant and direct influence on the decision to leave.

Finally, Job and Navy Dissatisfaction were two of the variables that showed an indirect effect on the decision to leave through their influence on the Civilian vs. Navy attitudinal variable. This pattern of results fits Fishbein and Ajzen's notion that Job and Navy dissatisfaction are expressions of attitudes toward objects and thus will affect intention and behavior only indirectly through their effect on the attitude toward the behavior. It is also compatible with, and explains, the results of the research on job satisfaction and job turnover that consistently shows only low correlations between the two variables (see review by Mobley et al., 1979).

It is equally important to note that some of the results of our analyses deviated from the Fishbein and Ajzen's model. According to their model behavioral intention, in our study conceived of as the decision to leave, is determined directly only by the attitude toward the behavior and the subjective norms. In contrast, our results showed that even when the attitudinal and subjective norms variable were included (Figure VI-1), the decision to leave has been influenced directly by three additional variables: Pay Grade, Job Simplicity, E, and Excess of Job Simplicity. It is also important to note that our path analyses did not include various strain measures, such as anxiety, that were shown to be correlated with and affected by stresses as seen in Table VI-1. These strains could have also shown a direct influence on the decision to leave, had they been measured well ahead of the decision and included in the analyses. Indeed, it has already been shown by Bentler and Speckart (1979; 1981) that, at least for certain types of behavior (e.g., drug use), variables other than attitude toward the behavior directly influence behavior. Future research should investigate the type of strains that influence intentions and behavior directly rather than being mediated by attitudes and subjective norms.

The present research points out that certain stresses and possibly various strains do influence behavior directly. It is theoretically plausible that stresses that create generalized strains (e.g., anxiety) tend to mask the perception of specific reinforcement contingencies that produce these strains. This might lead to a generalized force on the person to leave the field, yet, prevent the awareness and the formation of the cognitive elements (i.e., the behavioral beliefs about various consequences) that are part and parcel of the measurement and conceptualization of attitudes toward behavior.

Finally, let us point out that an important limitation of this study is the absence of direct and specific data on job performance. Attrition may be more of a problem to an organization if all of the worst performers stay and most of the best performers leave. Quite aside from its practical importance, we expect performance to play a role in future models of attrition. For example, it could be hypothesized that good performers will receive more social support from their supervisors, and a higher pay grade, which in turn will influence them to stay in the organization. In the Navy, for example, the good performer will also expect to receive more recognition in his career than he anticipates if he were to leave for a civilian job. This, too, is a factor which will influence him to stay. It is also important to note that the effect of job satisfaction on turnover is moderated by performance: job satisfaction keeps poor performers in the organization but has no such effect on good performers (Spencer & Steers, 1981).

CHAPTER VII

SUMMARY AND RECOMMENDATIONS FOR FUTURE RESEARCH

This chapter summarizes the findings on stress, social support, attrition, and on coping and defense. Finally, we suggest three research projects which are generated by the findings and theory in this project.

Summary of the Effects of Stress on Strain.

Hypothesis 1a asserts that stress increases strain. One test of this hypothesis, the cross-sectional partial correlations between stress and strain, showed the predicted positive correlations of Role Ambiguity and of Underutilization of Abilities with seven strains (Marital Dissatisfaction, Anxiety, Depression, Irritation, Somatic Complaints, Low Self-esteem and Job Dissatisfaction). Forty-seven out of a possible 70 correlations ranged from .08 to .45 (Table IV-3). On the other hand, Job Complexity and Work Load showed many fewer and weaker correlations; and unexpectedly most of them were negative. This suggests that many of these men were stressed by too little complexity and work load, and that a PE fit measure would be a better measure of stress for these variables. Further weak support for the effects of stress on strain came from analyses of the stresses of moving to a new residence and of low transferability of skills; both these stresses tended to be positively associated with one or two strains.

A longitudinal analysis of the effects of stress on strain supported both the findings in Table IV-3. Role Ambiguity and Underutilization of Abilities were positively but weakly correlated with strains whereas Job Complexity and Work Load showed weak negative correlations (Table IV-4).

Hypothesis 2a states: the worse the fit between the person and his environment, the greater the strain. The further question was raised whether the four different types of misfit (Good Fit, Poor Fit, Deficiency Fit, and Excess Fit) would have different effects. Cross-sectional multiple regressions provided results for 168 possible cells (4 fit measures x 3 dimensions of stress x 2 points in time x 7 strains); and 84 of these cells showed the predicted positive partial correlations (Table IV-7). Using the fit measures for the stress of Job Complexity we found, as suggested above, that all the correlations except one were positive, whereas using the environmental measure of stress, Job Complexity, E_s, the correlations were negative. Thus Hypothesis 2a was strongly supported. Each of the four types of misfit produces strain, but the patterns of the results are different. For Marital Stress, Excess Fit has the strongest effects on strain; and its opposite, Deficiency Fit, has no significant effects. On the other hand, for the stress of Job Complexity, Excess Fit and Deficiency Fit had equally strong effects on strains whereas Poor Fit had the strongest effects on strains.

According to Hypothesis 2b these measures of misfit will account for additional variance in strain over and above the additive effects of the component measures of E_s and P_s. This hypothesis is strongly supported (Table IV-8), with the amount of additional variance ranging from 1% to 8%. These latter results are consistent with tests of the hypothesis in several other studies.

There is weak support for the relevance hypothesis. Stresses in the work domain tend to affect most strongly strains which are also in the work domain such as Job Dissatisfaction. However, Marital Stress sometimes affects most strongly Marital Dissatisfaction but at other times it has stronger effects outside the domain of the marriage.

The theory and findings on acute stress, particularly the studies of stressful life events, suggest but do not prove that the <u>rate of increase</u> of stress has effects on strain over and above the effects of the <u>level</u> of stress. Our findings provide a weak test of this expectation and clearly support it for Underutilization of Abilities and for Role Ambiguity. It is not supported for Job Complexity, Work Load and Marital Stress (Table IV-9).

<u>Summary of the Effects of Social Support</u>.

Hypothesis 1 states that social support reduces stresses. The data in Table V-1 confirm this hypothesis for Job Complexity, Role Ambiguity, and Underutilization of Abilities. At least two of the three sources of support (Wife, Supervisor, Co-workers) are related to these stresses in both leavers and stayers. On the other hand, neither Work Load nor Marital Stress is related to social support in either group.

Hypothesis 2 asserts that social support reduces strains. This is true for each of the seven strains, for both wife support and supervisory support, and occurs for stayers and leavers at each of the three points in time (Table V-2). A longitudinal test of the hypothesis provided additional support (Table V-3).

An examination of Question 1, whether a change in social support will produce a corresponding change in strain, gave a qualified affirmative answer. The greater the increase in social support from the wife, the greater the decrease in Marital Dissatisfaction and in Depression. Other strains, i.e., Irritation, Somatic Complaints, Low Self-esteem showed trends in the same direction.

The prediction of person-environment fit theory, as applied to social support in Hypothesis 3, was confirmed (Table V-5). Misfit on social support from the wife accounts for additional variance in strain beyond the additive effects of its components, E_s and P_s.

In accordance with Hypothesis 4, we have found in most of our analyses that the more relevant the dependent strain is to the independent social support variable the stronger the effect.

The buffering of the effects of stress on strain by social support is complicated by the fact that both positive and negative buffering occur. When the measure of stress is E_s the cross-sectional tests for buffering yielded scattered findings with no clear patterns except that instances of significant buffering are much more often positive, 55 instances, than negative, 26 instances (see Appendix E). The longitudinal tests of the buffering hypothesis yielded similar but weaker results with a slight tendency toward more positive than negative buffering. It may well be that the longitudinal results are weaker than the cross-sectional because the time intervals were too long.

When the measure of stress is person-environment fit, there are about twice the expected number of instances of significant buffering; but in contrast to the findings for E_s, the buffering of F_s is predominantly negative. The ratios of positive to negative buffering are 10/19 for supervisor support and 8/12 for wife support.

The positive buffering of E_s compared to the negative buffering of F_s replicates our findings in a much more diverse sample (LaRocco et al., 1980). These differences may be due to the other component of F_s, namely P_s. In both data sets combined there were 37 significant correlations between P_s and strains, and all 37 of these were inverse. These main effects may be due to the effect of strain and stress on the adaptation of goals: continuing environmental deprivation leads to an adaptive lowering of goals. The interactive effects of P_s x supervisory support on strains are also negative, but they are weak. This suggests that social support from one's supervisor may facilitate the adaptation of goals.

Summary of the Determinants of Attrition.

The first step in the analysis correlated all the potential predictors with the attrition-retention variable. This resulted in 29 significant predictors whose correlations with attrition ranged from r=.08 to r=.34 (see Table VI-1).

The next step was to create a theoretical model utilizing only those variables thought to be direct or indirect causes of attrition. At this step we combined some single-item predictors into a more reliable index. For example, the men were asked to compare Navy jobs with civilian jobs on each of 10 desirable outcomes such as job security, respect, and friends, and these single items were combined into an index called "Navy vs. Civilian" with a coefficient alpha of .84. This step reduced the number of predictors from 29 to 10 or 11 for the two path analyses.

In the only sub-sample where it was used, the path analysis showed that the Navy vs. Civilian index was the strongest direct predictor of attrition. The leavers, compared to the stayers, expected more desirable outcomes in a civilian job. Other direct predictors of the decision to leave the Navy were: having a job low in complexity, a low pay grade, preferring a low work load, having less job complexity than desired, reporting low social support from one's supervisor, marital dissatisfaction, and a preference for low job complexity.

The path analyses revealed that other predictors had indirect effects on attrition via their effects on the direct predictors listed above. These indirect predictors included Underutilization of Abilities, Navy Dissatisfaction and Job Dissatisfaction in one path analysis, but these latter two measures of dissatisfaction had no effects on attrition in the other path analysis.

Suggestions for Further Research

A Secondary Analysis of Positive and Negative Buffering. The strongest findings in this study pertain to the main effects of social support in reducing stress, reducing strain and preventing attrition.

Unlike previous findings, however, the buffering effects are relatively weak. These findings are weak because social support sometimes reduces the effect of stress on strain, but social support sometimes increases the effect of stress on strain (i.e., negative buffering), so these opposing effects tend to cancel each other. The clearest opposition between positive and negative buffering occurs when we compare buffering of two different measures of stress: E_s and F_s. Buffering of E_s measures of stress yielded about twice as many instances of significant positive buffering as it did instances of significant negative buffering. In contrast, the buffering of F_s measures of stress yield predominantly negative buffering. Why this difference?

Since F_s yielded opposite effects to one of its components, E_s, it seemed reasonable that the difference was due to the other component, P_s. An examination of the interaction of P_s x social support from the supervisor revealed a negative partial correlation indicating that social support increases the effect of high goals in reducing strain. However, a reversed direction of causation for this cross-sectional finding seemed more plausible: high strain and stress cause people to adapt their goals for what they want in a job (P_s) downward to a more realistic level, and high social support facilitates this adaptation. This process could explain the occurrence of negative buffering in this ONR project and also in a previous project which found negative buffering by supervisory support when the measure of stress was F_s (LaRocco et al., 1980).

So the next step in research on positive and negative buffering should be a comparative analysis of these two large computerized data sets. The following questions could be addressed in one or the other or both data sets: 1) Is the negative relation between strain and the interaction P_s x social support, which we have found in the ONR data, also to be found in the other data set? 2) Will a longitudinal analysis support the interpretation that strain is the independent variable? 3) Will a longitudinal analysis support the interpretation that strain affects goals (P_s) more strongly than goals affect strain? 4) Will the answers to the first three questions vary when we examine separately: a) different sources of social support, b) different strains, c) different dimensions of stress, d) different measures of F_s (Good Fit, Poor Fit, Deficiency Fit, Excess Fit)?

This project should contribute substantially to our understanding of buffering. This in turn should eventually have important practical applications because positive buffering in the absence of negative buffering is potentially more efficient than the use of the main effects of social support. The provider of social support engages in social behaviors which entail some costs. If the same amount of social support is provided to all members of any group, and if it is equally effective with all members, then the outcome will produce main effects of social support. But if the amount of social support administered to each member is proportional to the amount of strain the member is suffering, then far less social support will be wasted by giving some members less social support than they need and giving other members more than they need. This more efficient use of social support would produce positive buffering. Similarly, for any given member the most efficient use of social support is to vary the dose over time as the person's strain varies. In short the understanding and control of buffering will enable us to utilize social support with those persons who need it most at the time that they need it most.

Extending the Study of Attrition. This research has produced some new and interesting findings on attrition even though it has some clear limitations. First, we have studied the decision to retire after it has been made. In our sample this decision may have been made many months before our data were collected - for some individuals perhaps even before enlistment. The factors determining the choice may be different early in a career from what they are after twenty years. Also the opportunities to influence attrition may be greater earlier in the career, and the best methods of influencing the decision may differ with length of service. We know from previous research that length of service is one of the best predictors of turnover: the longer the service, the lower the probability of leaving. So the findings of this study should be extended in a project which samples a wider range of length of service and which follows this sample over a longer period of time, involving three or four waves of data.

In such a project it would be appropriate to study the intention to retire in the future, a factor which could not be studied in our sample of men who had already made the decision to retire. We know from the studies of Bowers that the intention to retire is a good predictor of the actual decision (Bowers, 1975), and we would expect it to be the most immediate and direct cause of the decision. In any case the longitudinal design would strengthen the conclusions that can be drawn from the path analysis.

Another limitation of our study was the absence of data on job performance. Attrition may be more of a problem for the Navy if all of the worst performers stay and most of the best performers leave. Quite aside from its practical importance, we expect performance to play a role in our model of attrition. For example, we hypothesize that good performers will receive more social support from their supervisors which in turn will influence them to stay in the Navy. The good performer will also expect to receive more recognition in his Navy career than he anticipates if he were to leave for a civilian job. This, too, is a factor which will influence him to stay. Finally, we note that the effect of job satisfaction on turnover is moderated by performance: job satisfaction keeps poor performers in the organization but has no such effect on good performers (Spencer & Steers, 1981).

In summary, future research on attrition needs to test a comprehensive model of a dynamic process of career development and choice over the major phases of the career.

A Pilot Project on Improving the Quality of Working Life. In Chapter IV we have reported many significant findings about the effects of job stresses on strains. These findings are generally consistent with findings in other large organizations; so there is a body of dependable knowledge about how the quality of working life might be improved by reducing job stresses. But it is not always possible to eliminate or reduce all job stresses. However, Chapter V reports how the strains produced by intractable stress can be reduced by social support. Taken together the findings on stress and on social support provide the basis for designing a pilot project on improving the quality of working life in the Navy. The design of the project should provide for evaluating the difference between experimental and control groups using many of the same measures of stress, strain, and social support which have proved useful in this research. Two additional dependent variables should be added: measures of group effectiveness and cohesion.

REFERENCES

Ajzen, I., & Fishbein, M. Understanding attitudes and predicting social behavior. New Jersey: Prentice-Hall, 1980.

Ajzen, I., & Fishbein, M. Attitude-behavior relations: A theoretical analysis and review of empirical research. Psychological Bulletin, 1977, 84, 888-918.

Baekeland, F. & Lundwall, L. Dropping out of treatment: A critical review. Psychological Bulletin, 1975, 82, 738-783.

Bentler, P. M., & Speckart, G. Attitudes "cause" behaviors: A structural equation analysis. Journal of Personality and Social Psychology, 1981, 40, 226-238.

Bentler, P. M., & Speckart, G. Models of attitude-behavior relations. Psychological Review, 1979, 86, 452-464.

Bohrnstedt, G. W. Observations on the measurement of change. In F. Borgatta, (ed.), Sociological Methodology. San Francisco: Jossey-Bass, 1969.

Bowers, D. G. Organizational practices and the decision to reenlist. Institute for Social Research, 1973.

Bowers, D. G. Navy manpower: Values, practices and human resources requirements. Institute for Social Research, University of Michigan, 1975.

Bluedorn, A. C. A unified model of turnover from organizations. Human Relations, 1982a, 35, 135-153.

Bluedorn, A. C. The theories of turnover: Causes, effects and meaning. In S. Bacharach (Ed.) Perspectives in organizational sociology: Theory and Research (Vol. 1). Greenwich, Conn.: JAI, 1982b.

Caplan, R. D., Cobb, S., French, J. R. P., Jr., Harrison, R. V., & Pinneau, S. R., Jr. Job demands and worker health: Main effects and occupational differences. Ann Arbor: Institute for Social Research, 1980.

Caplan, R. D., Robinson, E. A. R., French, J. R. P., Jr., Caldwell, J. R. & Shinn, M. Adhering to medical regiments: Pilot experiments in patient education and social support. Institute for Social Research, University of Michigan: Ann Arbor, Michigan, 1976.

Cobb, S. Social support as a moderator of life stress. Psychosomatic Medicine, 1976, 38, 300-314.

Davidson, A., & Jaccard, J. Variables that moderate the attitude-behavior relation: Results of a longitudinal survey. Journal of Personality and Social Psychology, 1979, 37, 1364-1376.

Doehrman, S. R. Person-Environment Fit Theory, Social Support and Midlife Career Change. Presented at the 89th Annual Convention of the American Psychological Association, Los Angeles, California, August, 1981.

Drexler, J. A., Jr. Enlisted skill ratings, draft motivation, and the decision to reenlist. Institute for Social Research, 1975.

Drexler, J. A., Jr., & Bowers, D. G. Navy retention rates and human resources management. Technical Report, Institute for Social Research, 1973.

Fishbein, M., & Ajzen, I. Belief, attitude, intention, and behavior. Reading, Mass.: Addison-Wesley, 1975.

Fenichel, O. The psychoanalytic theory of neurosis. New York: Norton, 1945.

French, J. R. P., Jr., and Caplan, R. D., & Harrison, R. V. The mechanisms of job stress and strain. London: John Wiley, 1982.

French, J. R. P., Jr. and Doehrman, S. R. Increasing response rates to mail questionnaires: Effects of incentive and certified mail. Technical Report 1-1. Office of Naval Research, Organizational Effectiveness Research Program, 1980.

French, J. R. P., Jr., & Kahn, R. L. A programmatic approach to studying the industrial environment and mental health. Journal of Social Issues, 1962, 18, (3), 1-47.

French, J. R. P., Jr., Rodgers, W., & Cobb, S. Adjustment as person-environment fit. In G. V. Coelho, D. A. Hamburg, & J. E. Adams (Eds.), Coping and adaptation. New York: Basic Books, 1974.

Freud, A. Ego and the Mechanisms of Defense. International Universities Press: New York, 1946.

Gleser, G. C., & Ihilevich, D. An objective instrument for measuring defense mechanisms. Journal of Consulting and Clinical Psychology, 1969, 33, 51-60.

Harrison, R. V. Job Demands and Worker Health: Person-Environment Misfit. Doctoral dissertation, University of Michigan, 1976. University Microfilms No. 76-19150, 320 pages.

Harrison, R. V. Person-environment fit and job stress. In C. L. Cooper & R. Payne (Eds.), Stress at work. New York: John Wiley, 1977.

Hom, P. W., & Hulin, C. L. A competitive test of the prediction of reenlistment by several models. Journal of Applied Psychology, 1981, 66, 23-29.

House, J. S. The relationship of intrinsic and extrinsic work motivations to occupational stress and coronary heart disease risk (Doctoral dissertation, University of Michigan, 1972. Dissertation Abstracts International, 1972, 33, 2514-A. (University Microfilms No. 72-29094).

House, J. S. Work stress and social support. Reading, Mass.: Addison-Wesley, 1981.

House, J. S. & Wells, J. A. Occupational stress, social support and health. Proceedings of a Conference on Reducing Occupational Stress. Sponsored by Center for Occupational Mental Health, Cornell University and the National Institute of Occupational Safety and Health, White Plains, New York, May, 1978.

Joreskog, K. G., & Sorbom, D. G. LISREL IV: Estimation of linear structural equation systems by maximum likelihood methods. Chicago: National Educational Resources, 1978.

Kahle, L. R., & Berman, J. J. Attitudes cause behaviors: A cross-lagged panel analysis. Journal of Personality and Social Psychology, 1979, 37, 315-321.

Kroeber, T. C. The coping functions of the ego mechanisms. In R. White (Ed.), The study of lives. New York: Atherton Press, 1963.

LaRocco, J. M., House, J. S. & French, J. R. P., Jr. Social Support, occupational stress, and health. Journal of Health and Social Behavior, 1980, 21 (September): 202-218.

Lazarus, R. S., Averill, J. R., and Opton, E. M., Jr. The psychology of coping: Issues of research and assessment. In G. Coelho, D. Hamburg and S. Adams, ed., Coping and adaptation. New York: Basic Books, Inc., 1974.

Michaels, C. E., & Spector, P. E. Causes of employee turnover: A test of the Mobley, Griffeth, Hand, and Meglino model. Journal of Applied Psychology, 1982, 67, 53-59.

Miller, D. & Swanson, G. R. Inner Conflict and Defense, New York: Holt, 1960.

Mitchell, T. Expectancy models of job satisfaction, occupational preference, and effort. Psychological Bulletin, 1974, 81, 1053-1077.

Mitchell, T. R., & Biglan, A. Instrumentality theories: current uses in psychology. Psychological Bulletin, 1971, 76, 432-454.

Mobley, W., Griffeth, R., Hand, H., & Meglino, B. Review and conceptual analysis of the employee turnover process. Psychological Bulletin, 1979, 86, 493-522.

Nunnally, J. C. Psychometric Theory. McGraw Hill: New York, 1967.

Pinneau, S. R., Jr. Effects of social support on psychological and physiological strain. (Doctoral dissertation, University of

Michigan, 1975). Dissertation Abstracts International, 1976, 36, 5359B. (University Microfilms No. 76-9491).

Porter, L., & Steers, R. Organizational, work, and personal factors in employee turnover and absenteeism. Psychological Bulletin, 1973, 80, 151-176.

Rogosa, D. A critique of cross-lagged correlation. Psychological Bulletin, 1980, 88, 245-258.

Schlegel, R., Crawford, C., & Sanborn, M. Correspondence and mediational properties of the Fishbein model: An application to adolescent alcohol use. Journal of Experimental Social Psychology, 1977, 13, 421-430.

Schutz, W. C. The FIRO Scales Manual. Palo Alto, CA: Consulting Psychologists Press, 1967.

Sidle, A., Moos, R. H., Adams, J., and Cady, P. Development of a coping scale. Archives of General Psychiatry, 1969, 20, 225-232.

Spencer, D. G. and Steers, R. M. Performance as a moderator of the job satisfaction - turnover relationship. Journal of Applied Psychology, 1981, 66, 511-514.

Thurstone, L. L. The measurement of attitudes. Journal of Abnormal and Social Psychology, 1931, 26, 249-269.

Triandis, H. Interpersonal behavior. Monterey, Calif.: Brooks/Cole, 1977.

Vickers, R. Job stress, ego activity, and risk of coronary heart disease. (Doctoral dissertation, University of Michigan, 1979).

Vroom, V. H. Work and motivation. New York: Wiley, 1964.

APPENDIX A. Sample Cover Letter and additional information sheet

The University of Michigan
Research Center for Group Dynamics
Ann Arbor, Michigan 48106

A Division of the Institute
For Social Research

Dear Sir:

Not much attention has been paid to enlisted men like yourself who serve their country in the Navy for twenty or more years and then return to civilian life. There is little information available about how the transition from Navy to civilian life presents difficulties and how men successfully overcome the problems. The Office of Naval Research is supporting our project at the Institute for Social Research, University of Michigan, which will gather information from all twenty year, married, Navy enlisted men joining the Fleet Reserve in the next several months.

Although no individual's responses will ever be identified, we will provide summary findings to the Navy for their use in planning future retirement policies and programs. Also, at the end of the study we will send you reports of our findings which we believe will be of interest to you. People like youself that we have talked with in the past fifteen months have told us that our questions and their answers have given them a better perspective on their career change.

Enclosed are two questionnaires: the blue-covered one is to be filled out by you, and we also ask you wife to complete the pink-covered questionnaire. Since we want to look at the reactions of husbands and wives separately, please fill out the questionnaires in private. Then put each into its own large, postage-paid, envelope and return it to us.

To use your answers we must have your written permission and that of your wife. Therefore, complete the Privacy Act Statements, attached to the front of each questionnaire, and put both of them in the smaller white envelope. Mailing these statements separately from the questionnaire serves to protect the confidentiality of your answers. You and your wife are vital sources of information that can help people like yourself in the future and that can be of use to you now.

The attached page explains more details about the study.

Thank you very much for your cooperation.

Sincerely,

John R.P. French, Jr.
Program Director

ADDITIONAL INFORMATION ABOUT THE STUDY

What is the purpose of the study?

The primary purpose of this study is to gather information about the transition that a man passes through as he leaves the Navy and enters civilian life. We are focusing upon the man's Navy job, his home life and his new career. Preliminary research indicates that returning to civilian life and the civilian job market can be stressful for the Navy man and his family. We would like to find out more details about what people like you have to face and the steps you take in order to deal with this change. Also we will make recommendations to the Navy regarding its policies and programs for retirement so that men and women, like yourselves, may, in the future, have easier transitions to the civilian world.

Who is participating in the study?

We are currently asking all Navy men who are retiring from the Navy after 20 to 24 years of service, and their wives, to complete questionnaires. It is important that everyone who receives a questionnaire complete it. Otherwise, the conclusions we draw might be slanted and not reflect all the reactions to Navy "retirement."

What are we going to be asked to do?

We are asking you and your wife to complete the enclosed questionnaires now. In two months and again in eight months, we will ask each of you to complete another questionnaire much like the one you are filling out now. As our study is concerned with the changes in your life as you move from Navy life to civilian life, it is very important for you and your wife to complete questionnaires at these three selected points in time.

Will my views and those of my wife be kept confidential?

The study's findings will be presented only as statistical summaries. No individual's answers will ever be identified. Any identifying information will be kept separate from your answers.

What's in it for me?

We will send you reports of the study as soon as they become available. In addition, we hope you enjoy filling our our questionnaires. This study has been pre-tested and people who completed questionnaires in the pre-test indicated that they found the questionnaires very interesting and informative.

Who is conducting this study?

The study is being conducted by the Institute for Social Research, University of Michigan, Ann Arbor, Michigan. The project is supported by a grant (Contract Number N00014-78-C-0399) from the Office of Naval Research of the Department of the Navy. The Program Director for the study is Dr. John R.P. French (Ph.D.). Should you wish to contact him, please feel free to call him collect at (313) 764-8382 (Eastern Standard Time).

Appendix B

Description of measures of stress, social support, coping, defense, strain, effective coping, and demographics. The introduction (if any), content, and response scale of each measure are presented. An 'R' next to an item indicates that it was reverse scored.

Job complexity

(Note: Both the Job complexity E_s measure and P_s measure use the same introduction and item content but ask for different responses.)

Introduction:

WHAT DIFFERENT JOBS ARE LIKE

Please read what Don's job is like and what Dick's job is like. Then circle the number which describes the job you would prefer if you were looking for a new job. Follow the same procedure for each item in this section.

Item content:

	Don's Job	Dick's Job
1R.	Don's job has changes in work load; every once in a while Don has to work to his absolute maximum. When this happens he has to concentrate as hard as he can and be as careful as he can.	Dick's job goes along evenly from hour to hour and from day to day. The pace of the work stays about the same. He rarely, if ever, has to suddenly change the pace of his work and work even faster and harder.
	Tom's Job	Bob's Job
2R.	Tom's job requires him to be around people constantly. He works or talks with people most of the time.	Bob's job does not require him to work with anyone else. In his job Bob works alone. He rarely deals with other people.
	Rich's Job	Dan's Job
3R.	In Rich's job he works with people from several different groups. He has to handle each group differently because they have different needs and want to get different things done.	Dan's contact at work is strictly with the people in his own work group or department. He does not need to deal with several different groups or departments or organizations.

Response scale: Job complexity E_s and P_s use the following, different response scales. The proper names are changed to fit each item.

Job complexity, E_s scale:

MY JOB IS . . . (Circle One Number)

Exactly like Don's	A lot like Don's	Somewhat like Don's	Halfway Between Don's/Dick's	Somewhat like Dick's	A lot like Dick's	Exactly like Dick's
1	2	3	4	5	6	7

Job complexity P_s scale:

I WOULD PREFER A JOB . . . (Circle One Number)

Exactly like Don's	A lot like Don's	Somewhat like Don's	Halfway Between Don's/Dick's	Somewhat like Dick's	A lot like Dick's	Exactly like Dick's
1	2	3	4	5	6	7

Workload E_s

Introduction:

These questions deal with different aspects of work. Please rate these aspects of your typical work in the Navy over the last few years. Circle One Number Per Item.

Item Content:

1R. How much slow down in the work load do you experience?

2. How much work load do you have?

3R. How much time do you have to do all your work?

4. How many projects, assignments, or tasks do you have?

Response scale: One number was circled per item.

A Great Deal	A lot	Some	A little	Hardly Any
5	4	3	2	1

Workload P_s

(Note: two different versions of this measure were used with different subjects.)

Introduction: Version One

Realistically think of yourself in your Navy job over the last few years. Circle One Number Per Item.

Item Content:

1. How much work load can you handle?

2R. How much time do you need to do all your work adequately?

3. How many projects, assignments, or tasks can you do well?

4R. How much slow down in the work load do you require to work best overall?

Introduction: Version Two

If you were designing a job for yourself, how much of each of the following would you like to have in such a job? (CIRCLE ONE NUMBER PER ITEM)

Item Content:

1. How much work load would you like to have?

2R. How much time would you like to have to do all your work?

3. How many projects, assignments, or tasks would you like to have?

4R. How much slow down in the work load would you prefer?

Response scale: Both versions of Workload P_s used the same response scale as was used for Workload E_s.

Role ambiguity E_s.

Introduction:

These questions deal with different aspects of work. Please indicate how often these aspects appear in your job. Circle One Number Per Item.

Item Content:

1R. How often are you clear on what your responsibilities are?

2R. How much of the time are your work objectives well defined?

3R. How often are you clear about what others expect of you on the job?

Response scale: One number was circled per item.

Very often	Fairly often	Some-times	Occa-sionally	Rarely
5	4	3	2	1

Role ambiguity P_s

Introduction:

Here are some items which describe different aspects of jobs. If you could have your own way about designing a job for yourself, how would you like each of the following to be? Circle One Number Per Item.

Item Content:

1R. How often would you like to be clear on what others expect of you on the job?

2R. How often would you like to be clear on what your job responsibilities are?

3R. How much of the time would you like your work objectives to be well-defined?

Response scale: The same as was used for Role ambiguity E_s.

Underutilization of abilities

Introduction:

This next set of items deals with the use of your skills and abilities. Indicate how often you use each type. Circle One Number Per Item.

Item Content:

1R. How often does your job let you use the skills and knowledge you learned in Navy training schools?

2R. How often are you given a chance to do the things you do best?

Response scale: One number was circled per item.

Rarely	Occasionally	Sometimes	Fairly often	Very often
1	2	3	4	5

Non-transferability of skills

Introduction:

The following questions are concerned with how useful your Navy training and experience has been in your current job.

Item Content:

1R. How often are the managerial and supervisory skills and training you received in the Navy useful in your current job?

2R. How often are the technical and occupational skills and training you received in the Navy useful in your current job?

3. Regardless of your current job, do you feel the skills you learned in your Navy job specialty are transferable to a civilian job?

   a. Managerial/Supervisory Skills

   b. Technical/Occupational Skills

Response scales: One number was circled per item.

For items 1 and 2:	Seldom	Occasionally	Fairly Often	Very Often	Always
	1	2	3	4	5

For items 3a. and b.	Highly Transferable	Somewhat Transferable	Slightly Transferable	Not At All Transferable
	1	2	3	4

Inequity of pay

Item Content:

1R. Compared to Navy people who do a similar job to yours, how fair is your pay and benefits?

2R. Compared to civilian people who have similar skills to yours, how fair is your pay and benefits?

3R. Compared to civilian people who do a job similar to yours, how fair is your pay and benefits?

Response scale: One number was circled per item.

Very Much Less Than I Ought To Get	Somewhat Less Than I Ought To Get	A Little Less Than I Ought To Get	About The Same As I Ought To Get	More Than I Ought To Get
1	2	3	4	5

Marital stress E_s

Introduction:

From your perspective, how much of each of the following family related activities/tasks does your wife feel you should do in a typical, recent week?

Item Content:

1. taking care of children

2. doing odd jobs around the house

3. showing affection for your wife

Response scale: One number was circled per item.

None or very Little	A Little	Some	A lot	A Great Deal
1	2	3	4	5

Marital Stress Ps

Introduction:

Considering both what you ought to do and what you feel like doing, how much of each of the following family related tasks/activities are you willing to do in a typical, recent week?

Item Content:

1. taking care of children
2. doing odd jobs around the house
3. showing affection for your wife

Response scale: One number was circled per item.

None or very Little	A Little	Some	A lot	A Great Deal
1	2	3	4	5

Navy vs. civilian life

Introduction:

Below is a list of factors which many Navy enlisted men consider when deciding to stay in the Navy after 20 years or to leave the Navy for a civilian job. For each factor, please indicate whether you think the factor would be better for you in a Navy job or better for you in a civilian job. Circle One Number Per Item.

Item Content:

1. Opportunity for making friends at work
2. Opportunity for leisure time with your family
3. Potential work-related physical hazards
4. Potential rewards for job performance
5. Opportunity for paid travel
6. Fringe benefits
7. Opportunity for desired overtime
8. Opportunity to develop new skills
9. Opportunity for high salary
10. Opportunity for desired amount of responsibility at work
11. Potential for nondesired, required overtime
12. Potential respect for your past Navy experience
13. Discipline and rules of workplace
14. Chance to share home tasks with your wife
15. Job security
16. Quality of leadership supervisor
17. Opportunity to utilize your major skills

Response Scale: One number was circled per item.

Clearly better in a Navy job	Somewhat better in a Navy job	About the same	Somewhat better in a civilian job	Clearly better in a civilian job
1	2	3	4	5

Social support, supervisor and co-worker

Introduction and item content:

PEOPLE AROUND YOU IN THE NAVY

1. How much will each of these people go out of their way to do things to make your work life easier?

   A. Your immediate supervisor (boss)

   B. Other people at work

2. How easy is it to talk with each of the following people when you want to?

   A. Your immediate supervisor

   B. Other people at work

3. How much are you able to rely on these people when things get tough at work?

   A. Your immediate supervisor

   B. Other people at work

Response scale: One number was circled per item.

For items 1 and 3 above:	Very much	Some-what	A little	Not at all
	4	3	2	1

For item 2 above:	Very easy	Easy	Difficult	Very Difficult
	4	3	2	1

Social Support Wife E_s

Introduction: Below is a list of many types of support that a wife can provide. How much does your wife actually do each of the following?

Item Content:

1. do things she thinks will make you happy?
2. say and do things that improve relations with you?
3. try to do things to make you feel loved?
4. do things for you around the house
5. say and do things that shows she understands your feelings about things?
6. say and do things to try and raise your self-confidence about the future?

Response scale: One number was circled per item.

None or very little	A little	Some	A lot	A Great Deal
1	2	3	4	5

Social Support Wife P_s

Introduction:

Below is a list of many types of support that a wife can provide. How much support should a wife provide in order for it to be just right?

How much should she:

Item content: Same items as Social Support E_s.

Response scale: The same as was used for Social Support E_s.

Anxiety, Depression, Irritation

(Note: The three affective strains of anxiety, depression, and irritation were presented under the same introduction, with items relevant to one of the strains intermingled with items relevant to the other two strains. The numbers adjacent to the items in the following scales indicate their position in the affective strain question list.)

Introduction:

HOW I FEEL THESE DAYS

Here are some items about how people may feel. When you think about your feelings during the past two weeks, how much of the time do you feel this way? Circle One Number Per Item.

Item Content:

Anxiety

2. I feel nervous.

5. I feel jittery.

6R. I feel calm.

11. I feel fidgety.

Depression

1R. I feel good.

4. I feel sad.

8. I feel unhappy.

10. I feel depressed.

12. I feel blue.

13R. I feel cheerful.

Irritation

3. I feel angry.

7. I feel aggravated.

9. I feel irritated.

14. I feel annoyed.

Response scale: The following was used for items pertaining to each of the three affective strains. One number was circled per item.

Never or A little of the Time	Some of the Time	A Good Part of the Time	Most of the Time
1	2	3	4

Alcohol use

Introduction:

The following questions ask about how much you have to drink on the occasions when you drink alcoholic beverages. From these questions, a "drink" means any of the following:

a 12 ounce can (or bottle) of beer
a 4 ounce glass of wine
a mixed drink or shot glass of liquor

Item Content:

1. During the last 30 days, on how many occasions (if any) have you had alcohol to drink?

2. Think back over the last two weeks. How many times have you had five or more drinks in a row?

3. During the last two weeks, how many times have you had 3 or 4 drinks in a row (but no more than that)?

Response scale: One choice was selected per item.

For item one: 0, 1-2, 3-5, 6-9, 10-19, 20-30, 40 or more occasions.

For items two and three: None, once, twice, 3 to 5 times, 6 to 9 times, 10 or more times.

Obesity

The man's height in feet and inches was requested as was his weight in pounds. Obesity is defined as the ratio of the weight to the square of the height.

Somatic complaints

Introduction:

Have you experienced any of the following during the past month? Circle One Number Per Item.

Item Content:

1. Your hands trembled enough to bother you.
2. You were bothered by shortness of breath when you were not working hard or exercising
3. You were bothered by your heart beating hard
4. Your hands sweated so that you felt damp and clammy
5. You had spells of dizziness
6. You were bothered by having an upset stomach or stomach ache
7. You were bothered by your heart beating faster than usual
8. You were in ill health which affected your work
9. You had a loss of appetite
10. You had trouble sleeping at night

Response scale: One number was circled per item.

Never	Once or Twice	Three or More Times
1	2	3

Ill health

Item content:

How would you rate your overall health during the past two months?

Response scale: One number was circled.

Very Outstanding	Outstanding	Excellent	Very Good	Good	Fair	Poor	Very Poor
1	2	3	4	5	6	7	8

Marital dissatisfaction

(Note: This scale contained two sets of items with different response scales. The second set, but not the first, had an introduction)

Item Content:

1R. How often do you discuss or have you considered divorce, separation, or terminating your relationship?

2. In general, how often do you think that things between you and your wife are going well?

3R. Do you ever regret that you married?

Introduction (to the second set of items).

How often would you say the following events occur between you and your mate?

Item Content:

4R. Laugh together

5R. Calmly discuss something

6R. Work together on a project

Response scale: One number was circled per item.

First set of items:	All the time	Most of the time	More Often than not	Occa- sionally	Rarely	Never
	1	2	3	4	5	6

Second set of items:	Never	Less than Once a Month	Once or Twice a Month	Once or Twice a Week	Once a Day	More
	1	2	3	4	5	6

Low self esteem

Introduction:

Circle the number which best describes how you see yourself.

Item Content:

1. As a worker on your job
2. As a provider for your family
3. As a husband
4. As a father

Response scale: One number was circled per item.

Successful						Not Successful
1	2	3	4	5	6	7

Job dissatisfaction

(Note: Each of the three items composing this measure has a different response scale. To facilitate the presentation, the response scale for each item is presented immediately after its content.)

Introduction:

These questions have to do with your attitude toward the job (rating) you have and the work you do in the Navy.

Item content and response scale:

1. Knowing what you know now, if you had to decide all over again whether to take the type of job you now have, what would you decide?

I WOULD...

1	2	3
Decide without hesitation to take the same type of job	Have some second thoughts	Decide definitely not to take this type of job

2. If a friend of yours told you he was interested in working in a job like yours, what would you tell him?

I WOULD...

1	2	3
Strongly recommend it	Have doubts about recommending it	Advise him against it

3. All in all, how satisfied would you say you are with your job?

1	2	3	4	5
Very satisfied	Somewhat satisfied	Indifferent	Not too satisfied	Not at all satisfied

Navy dissatisfaction

Introduction:

These questions have to do with your general attitude toward the Navy.

Item content:

1. Knowing what you know now, if you had to decide all over again whether to join the Navy, what would you decide?
2. If a friend of yours told you he was interested in joining the Navy, what would you tell him?
3. All in all, how satisfied would you say you are with the Navy?

Response scales: One number was circled per item.

1.

1	2	3
Decide without hesitation to join	Have some second thoughts	Decide definitely not to join

2 and 3. The response scales for these items are identical to those for items 2 and 3, respectively, of the job dissatisfaction measure.

Effective coping - school.

Introduction:

In terms of going to school, have you (Answer each item):

Item Content:

1. Talked seriously with friends about your educational plans
2. Discussed educational plans thoroughly with relations
3. Talked with an academic counselor
4. Decided upon your major subject
5. Applied to a school
6. Been accepted at a school
7. Currently enrolled in a school
8. Finished an academic curriculum in the past two years
9. Applied for the GI Bill

Response scale: The respondent checked either 'yes' or 'no' after each item.

Effective coping - work.

Introduction:

In terms of going to work, have you (Answer each item):

Item content:

1. Talked with friends oı relatives
2. Talked with a job counselor
3. Prepared a resume
4. Searched through job listings
5. Contacted employment agencies
6. Interviewed for a job(s)
7. Been offered a firm job position
8. Accepted or begun working at a job you plan to continue temporarily after you leave the Navy
9. Accepted or begun working at a job you plan to continue permanently after you leave the Navy
10. Applied for unemployment benefits

Response scale: the respondent checked either 'yes' or 'no' after each item.

Demographic information

(Note: In addition to requesting age, years of marriage, and number of children, the following measures were collected.)

Education

Item content:

1. Less than 12 years
2. General Equivalency Diploma (GED)
3. High school graduate
4. A.A. degree
5. BA/BS degree
6. Advanced degree, e.g., M.A.

Response scale: One of the six choices was checked.

Paygrade

Item content:

Paygrade E - ___

Response scale: A number from five to nine, representing the possible paygrade classifications of twenty year Navy enlisted men, was entered.

Rate

Item content: Rate: ___

Response scale: The respondent entered a three to four letter code signifying his job classification in the Navy.

Navy program suggestions:

(Note: The following was collected from retirees to provide information to the Navy. The responses were not used to test any theoretical hypotheses or research questions.)

Introduction:

Listed below are a number of conceivable programs and services for Navy enlisted men entering civilian life after at least twenty years of service. For each item, please indicate how useful you think it would be for you in getting a job after you leave the Navy. Circle One Number Per Item.

Item content:

1. Job aptitude testing
2. Information booklets about Navy pension benefits
3. Lists of Navy retirees at different geographical locations
4. Job counseling programs for post-Navy employment
5. Involvement of wifes in retirment programs and seminars
6. Retirement counseling groups headed by recent Navy retirees
7. Job placement service
8. Job training courses for alternative careers
9. Initiation of support programs at least six months before Navy separation
10. Continuation of support programs at least six months after Navy separation

Response scale: One number was circled per item.

Won't help me get the kind of job I want	Will slightly improve the chances of getting the kind of job I want	Will somewhat improve the chances of getting the kind	Will improve alot the chances of getting the kind of job I want	Will greatly improve the chances of getting the kind of job I want
1	2	3	4	5

Coping and Defense

Introduction

The next few pages describe issues with which many retiring Navy men have to deal. Read each paragraph. Imagine the situation described as if it were really happening to you. Then respond to the items which follow the paragraph according to what your reaction would be if you were the person in the situation. Pick the location along the five points according to your feeling at the moment. Choose one number and circle it. Work through these items at a steady pace without dwelling on any one of them.

(Note: A total of six paragraphs describing six different vignettes were presented. After each vignette, the subject was to respond about several possible reactions, each of which corresponded to a coping or defensive disposition. Below are provided (in order): the six vignettes, the possible reactions which pertain to each disposition, and the response scale. The number next to each reaction corresponds to the vignette to which it pertains.)

Item Content for vignettes:

1. You will soon be retiring from the Navy. Last weekend you and your wife argued about what type of job you should be looking for. She urges you to take the first decent job that brings in an adequate income, but you are willing to put up with five or six months of economic hardship while you look for an interesting job with a future.

2. You are planning to retire from the Navy in a month. Very unexpectedly, the Navy needs someone with exactly your skills and experience. Yesterday, they called to offer you a three-year reenlistment package including shore duty, a 15% salary (pro-pay) increase and some new responsibilities you had asked for sometime ago - everything, in fact, that you want. The Navy wants your answer in two days.

3. You are about to retire from the Navy. Yesterday you and your wife got into a disagreement about plans for the future and you said, "After twenty years in the service I've been expecting some attention at home when I retire." She replied, "Well after all these years as a Navy wife I think I deserve a little extra consideration myself."

4. You are about to retire from the Navy. A few months ago the brother-in-law of one of your Navy buddies offered you a job in his machine shop. This was just the job you wanted, so you accepted and then stopped looking into other jobs. You were supposed to start working in two weeks, but yesterday your "employer" called you and said, "Business has been very slow lately so I guess I won't be able to hire you after all. Sorry it didn't work out."

5. You will be retiring from the Navy soon and you've lined up a job with an insurance company where you supervise five clerical workers who are employed part-time. They don't seem to respect your skills or background. Yesterday, when you visited the company to finalize your job plans you overheard your future subordinates saying, "I'm afraid what he's learned in the Navy won't be of much use here" and "it's going to take him quite a while to learn the job."

6. You are about to retire from the Navy and you've made plans to go to college for a year and work toward a degree in business. Classes begin in two weeks and you've already set up your class schedule and bought some of your books. When you start looking through them you realize it's going to be very difficult—you've forgotten a lot of what you learned in high school and most of the material seems way over your head.

Item content for defensive processes

Constriction of negative affect

1R. Bill isn't upset about this argument.

3R. Jay isn't upset about this disagreement.

4R. Pete isn't upset about losing the job.

5R. Bill isn't upset about his subordinates' comments.

6R. Tom isn't upset about starting school.

Reversal

2R. George is pleased that the Navy finally offered him the type of job he would like.

3R. Van is glad that they have the opportunity to solve this problem now rather than have it crop up later.

4R. Gary is content to have the opportunity to change his plans. He might not have liked the job anyway.

5R. Bob is pleased to be able to work with a group who will wait before they evaluate him.

6R. Nate thinks it will be good to have the chance to deal with a challenge so soon after retirement.

Intellectualism

1R. Steve thinks that this conflict is probably a result of the difficulty caused by a major career change.

3R. Mark thinks people generally have trouble adjusting to career changes.

4R. Jay concludes that small businesses may not provide much job security.

5R. Mike decides that it takes all supervisors time to adjust to a new work group.

6R. Don believes that people returning to school pass through a readjustment period.

Displacement - other

1R. Bud wishes his wife would help make his job hunt easier.

2R. Al is annoyed that the Navy made him the offer at such an inconvenient time.

4R. Tim is frustrated that the "employer" put him in such a bind.

5R. Gary is irked that his people are judging him before he's even started work.

6R. George wishes the school counselor had told him that returning to school after several years' absence isn't easy.

Displacement - self

1R. Bob wishes he'd been able to find a good job for himself by now.

2R. Ed regrets that he didn't get the offer earlier before he got involved in leaving the Navy.

3R. Jim blames himself for not seeing the problem coming and doing something about it before now.

4R. Joe is very annoyed at himself for putting all his eggs in one basket when he could have been exploring other alternatives.

6R. Irv is disappointed with himself for not being better prepared.

Distorted Locus - Control

2. Hal feels that what he does will completely determine his job future.

3. Frank feels that what he does will completely determine the resolution of the disagreement.

4. Gene feels that what he does will completely determine his locating a good job.

5. Rich feels that what he does will completely determine his satisfaction with his new job.

6. Rick feels that what he does now will completely determine how well he does in school.

Item content for coping processes[1]

Mastery of environmental demands.

1R. Mark asks his wife to give him time and not expect much from him for a while.

2R. Dave asks for more time to make his decision.

5R. Van suggests to his group that they give him a chance to learn the job before evaluating him.

6R. John arranges to take a lighter class load.

Mastery of environmental supplies.

1. Charlie asks his wife to help him with his job search.

2. Tom asks the Navy to put the details of the offer in writing.

4. Jim asks his wife and some friends for help in his new job search.

5. Joe asks his friends about other career possibilities in case this job doesn't work out.

Adaptation of Motives.

1R. Eric thinks about scaling down his job plans, at least for the time being.

3R. George thinks he might have to do without special attention at home for awhile.

6R. Ernie thinks that he may not do as well as he'd expected, at least during his first semester.

Adaptation of Abilities.

4R. Al signs up for a job training program which will qualify him for more jobs.

5R. Don spends his evenings reading up on the insurance business.

6R. Steve starts prepaing for school with an intensive review of his high school textbooks.

[1]Items were scored in the downward direction, i.e., the greater the score, the more the person was using coping downward.

Response scale for coping and defensive processes:

My reaction would be:

1	2	3	4	5
Exactly like (name)	A lot like (name)	Somewhat like (name)	Slightly like (name)	Not at all like (name)

APPENDIX C. Zero-order correlations among the major variables in the study. Subjects are leavers at time 1.

	Job Comp. P_s	Job Comp. E_s	Job Comp. GF	Work-Load E_s	Role Ambiguity P_s	Role Ambiguity E_s	Role Ambiguity GF	Under-utiliz. of Abilities	Marital Stress P_s	Marital Stress E_s	Marital Stress GF
<u>Stress</u>											
Job Complexity E_s	.31**										
Job Complexity GF	-.62	.56**									
Work Load E_s	.03	.33**	.25**								
Role Ambiguity P_s	.01	-.01	-.01	.10*							
Role Ambiguity E_s	-.07	-.13**	-.04	-.00	.06						
Role Ambiguity GF	-.06	-.09*	-.02	-.07	-.73**	.64**					
Underutilization of Abilities E_s	-.12**	-.18**	-.05	-.16**	-.08*	.29**	.26**				
Marital Stress P_s	.10**	.09*	-.01	.00	-.07	-.03	.03	-.09*			
Marital Stress E_s	.08*	-.00	-.07	.00	-.08*	.02	.08*	-.06	.50**		
Marital Stress GF	-.03	-.10**	-.05	.00	-.01	.05	.04	.03	-.58**	.41**	
<u>Social Support</u>											
Social Support Supervisor	.05	.08*	.02	-.04	.04	-.35**	-.27**	-.23**	.05	-.02	-.07
Social Support Coworker	.10	.08	-.03	.07	.01	-.30**	-.22**	-.15*	.14*	.05	-.09
Social Support Wife P_s	.11**	.08*	-.03	.03	-.15**	-.00	.11**	-.07	.19**	.17**	-.05
Social Support Wife E_s	.11**	.15**	.03	.07	-.03	-.07	-.03	-.11**	.29**	.04	-.28**
Social Support Wife GF	.03	.10*	.06	.05	.07	-.07	-.10**	-.06	.16**	-.08*	-.24**

*$p < .05$
**$p < .01$

APPENDIX C. (Cont'd.) Zero-order correlations among the major variables in the study. Subjects are leavers at time 1.

Strain	Job Comp. P_s	Job Comp. E_s	Job Comp. GF	Work-Load E_s	Role Ambiguity P_s	Role Ambiguity E_s	Role Ambiguity GF	Under-utiliz. of Abilities	Marital Stress P_s	Marital Stress E_s	Marital Stress GF
Marital Dissatisfaction	-.03	-.11**	-.07	-.03	-.11**	.06	.13**	.09*	-.30**	-.05	.28**
Anxiety	-.02	.00	.02	.03	-.12**	.08*	.14**	.10**	-.04	.01	.05
Depression	-.10**	.01	.09*	-.02	-.04	.21**	.17**	.14**	-.11	-.02	.10**
Irritation	-.09*	.07	.13**	.03	-.08*	.19**	.19**	.11**	-.06	.00	.06
Somatic Complaints	-.02	.06	.07	.04	-.03	.09*	.08*	.05	-.01	.01	.02
Low Self-esteem	-.05	-.06	-.00	-.04	-.08*	.09*	.12**	.13**	-.13**	-.00	.14**
Job Dissatisfaction	-.16**	-.10*	.07	-.09*	-.02	.21**	.16**	.38**	-.01	.03	.03

*$p < .05$
**$p < .01$

APPENDIX C. (Cont'd.) Zero-order correlations among the major variables in the study. Subjects are leavers at time 1.

	Social Support Supervis.	Social Support Coworker	Social Support Wife P_s	Social Support Wife E_s	Social Support Wife GF	Marital Dissat.	Anxiety	Depression	Irritation	Somatic Compl.	Low Self esteem
<u>Social Support</u>											
Social Support Coworker	.32**										
Social Support Wife P_s	-.01	.02									
Social Support Wife E_s	.03	.15*	.38**								
Social Support Wife GF	.04	.13*	-.36**	.73**							
<u>Strain</u>											
Marital Dissatisfaction	-.08	-.11	-.09*	-.62**	-.55**						
Anxiety	-.11**	-.17**	.06	-.11**	-.16**	.21**					
Depression	-.12**	-.25**	-.05	-.27**	-.23**	.30**	.59**				
Irritation	-.13**	-.27**	-.00	-.18**	-.18**	.19**	.48**	.70**			
Somatic Complaints	-.09*	-.10	.09*	.01	-.05	.09*	.43**	.37**	.28**		
Low Self-esteem	-.07	-.07	-.09*	-.39**	-.33**	.43**	.27**	.26**	.20**	.14**	
Job Dissatisfaction	-.17**	-.19**	-.05	-.09*	-.05	.05	.12**	.20**	.22**	.13**	.15**

* $p < .05$
**$p < .01$

APPENDIX D. Zero-order correlations among the major variables in the study. Subjects are stayers at time 1.

	Job Comp. P_s	Job Comp. E_s	Job Comp. GF	Work-Load E_s	Role Ambiguity P_s	Role Ambiguity E_s	Role Ambiguity GF	Under-utiliz. of Abilities	Marital Stress P_s	Marital Stress E_s	Marital Stress GF
Stress											
Job Complexity E_s	.33**										
Job Complexity GF	-.69**	.47**									
Work Load E_s	.14*	.42**	.20**								
Role Ambiguity P_s	-.11	-.19**	-.04	-.08							
Role Ambiguity E_s	-.16*	-.10	.07	-.07	.03						
Role Ambiguity GF	-.02	.08	.08	.01	-.77**	.62**					
Underutilization of Abilities	-.21**	-.25**	-.00	-.18**	.06	.34**	.18**				
Marital Stress P_s	.11	.16*	.02	.02	-.09	-.12	-.01	-.16*			
Marital Stress E_s	.10	.11	-.01	.11	-.03	-.20**	-.11	-.16*	.41**		
Marital Stress GF	-.04	-.07	-.02	.10	.06	-.05	-.08	.03	-.64**	.44**	
Social Support											
Social Support Supervisor	.18**	.13	-.07	-.06	.01	-.23**	-.15	-.32**	.17*	.10	-.09
Social Support Coworker	.16*	.04	-,.12	-.08	-.07	-.16*	-.05	-.07	.18**	-.01	-.18**
Social Support Wife P_s	.09	.11	-.00	.01	-.17*	-.02	.12	-.20**	.22**	.13	-.12
Social Support Wife E_s	.13	.02	-.10	.09	-.07	-.10	-.01	-.29**	.25**	.12	-.14*
Social Support Wife GF	.07	-.05	-.11	.09	.04	-.10	-.10	-.17	.09	.04	-.06

*$p < .05$
**$p < .01$

APPENDIX D (Cont'd.) Zero-order correlations for stayers at time 1.

	Social Support Supervis.	Social Support Coworker	Social Support Wife P_s	Social Support Wife E_s	Social Support Wife GF	Marital Dissat.	Anxiety	Depression	Irritation	Somatic Compl.	Low Self esteem
<u>Social Support</u>											
Social Support Coworker	.27**										
Social Support Wife P_s	.04	.08									
Social Support Wife E_s	.19**	.23**	.44**								
Social Support Wife GF	.18**	.19**	-.26**	.75**							
<u>Strain</u>											
Marital Dissatisfaction	-.18**	-.23**	-.15*	-.70**	-.64**						
Anxiety	-.28**	-.09	.01	-.23**	-.26**	.10					
Depression	-.32**	-.19**	.02	-.09	-.11	.12	.50**				
Irritation	-.34**	-.16*	-.01	-.10	-.11	.13	.38**	.50**			
Somatic Complaints	-.04	-.09	.19**	-.02	-.17*	.08	.17*	.23**	.20**		
Low Self-esteem	-.19**	-.23**	-.17*	-.42**	-.34**	.39**	.18**	.14*	.10	.15*	
Job Dissatisfaction	-.26**	-.16*	-.04	-.12	-.11	.07	.09	.36**	.25**	.13	.21**

* $p < .05$
**$p < .01$

APPENDIX D (Cont'd.) Zero-order correlations for stayers at time 1.

Strain	Job Comp. P_s	Job Comp. E_s	Job Comp. GF	Work-Load E_s	Role Ambiguity P_s	Role Ambiguity E_s	Role Ambiguity GF	Under-utiliz. of Abilities	Marital Stress P_s	Marital Stress E_s	Marital Stress GF
Marital Dissat.	-.12	-.02	.10	-.01	.06	.10	.02	.20**	-.25**	-.09	.17*
Anxiety	-.02	.10	.10	.01	.07	.11	.02	.10	-.03	-.02	-.00
Depression	-.13	-.01	.12	.03	-.10	.10	.14*	.17*	-.16*	-.04	.09
Irritation	.00	.06	.05	.16*	-.11	.09	.15*	.02	-.18**	-.04	.13
Somatic Complaints	-.01	.11	.09	.06	-.10	.02	.09	.02	-.06	.00	.04
Low Self-esteem	-.11	-.10	.02	.03	.06	.20**	.08	.19**	-.19**	-.08	.13
Job Dissatisfaction	-.14*	-.10	-.05	.01	-.07	-.14*	.15*	.23**	-.11	-.06	-.07

*p < .05
**p < .01

APPENDIX E. The buffering effects of social support upon the stress-strain relationship. The findings were from cross-sectional ordered multiple regressions. Dependent variable was strain. The order of predictors was: stress, social support, stress x social support. Controls were education and pay grade. Entries provide the amount of direction of the partial correlation between stress x social support and strain, controlling on preceeding predictors. A negative correlation indicates positive buffering; a positive correlation indicates negative buffering. Social support was either: Wife E_s (Wi E_s), Wife Deficiency Fit (Wi DE), or Supervisor E_s (Su E_s).

Stayers at time 1.

Strains	Marital Dissatisfaction			Anxiety			Depression			Irritation			Somatic Complaints			Low Self-esteem			Job Dissatisfaction		
Social Supports / Stresses	Wi E_s	Wi DE	Su E_s	Wi E_s	Wi DE	Su E_s	Wi E_s	Wi DE	Su E_s	Wi E_s	Wi DE	Su E_s	Wi E_s	Wi DE	Su E_s	Wi E_s	Wi DE	Su E_s	Wi E_s	Wi DE	Su E_s
Job Complexity		+.15**																	-.14**		
Work Load																	-.14**		-.14*		
Role Ambiguity	-.16**																	-.12*	-.12*		
Underutilization of Abilities						-.12*										+.13*					-.12*
Marital Stress			+.14**																		

Stayers at time 3.

Strains	Marital Dissatisfaction			Anxiety			Depression			Irritation			Somatic Complaints			Low Self-esteem			Job Dissatisfaction		
Social Supports / Stresses	Wi E_s	Wi DE	Su E_s	Wi E_s	Wi DE	Su E_s	Wi E_s	Wi DE	Su E_s	Wi E_s	Wi DE	Su E_s	Wi E_s	Wi DE	Su E_s	Wi E_s	Wi DE	Su E_s	Wi E_s	Wi DE	Su E_s
Job Complexity				-.16*			-.14*							-.15*						-.14*	
Work Load				-.17**																	
Role Ambiguity										-.15*			+.14*	+.15*			+.15*				
Underutilization of Abilities				-.20**			-.17**		-.17**	-.16*								+.18**		+.14*	
Marital Stress				+.18**											-.24***						

$*p < .10$; $**p < .05$; $***p < .01$

APPENDIX E (Cont'd.)

Leavers at time 1.

Strains	Marital Dissatisfaction			Anxiety			Depression			Irritation			Somatic Complaints			Low Self-esteem			Job Dissatisfaction		
Social Supports / Stresses	Wi E_s	Wi DE	Su E_s	Wi E_s	Wi DE	Su E_s	Wi E_s	Wi DE	Su E_s	Wi E_s	Wi DE	Su E_s	Wi E_s	Wi DE	Su E_s	Wi E_s	Wi DE	Su E_s	Wi E_s	Wi DE	Su E_s
Job Complexity											-.07*						+.08**		+.07*		
Work Load													-.07*							+.07*	-.08*
Role Ambiguity												-.07*			+.08**				+.07*	+.08**	
Underutilization of Abilities				+.07*													-.07*				
Marital Stress	-.12***	-.08**								+.06							+.08*	+.09**			

Leavers at time 2.

Strains	Marital Dissatisfaction			Anxiety			Depression			Irritation			Somatic Complaints			Low Self-esteem			Job Dissatisfaction		
Social Supports / Stresses	Wi E_s	Wi DE	Su E_s	Wi E_s	Wi DE	Su E_s	Wi E_s	Wi DE	Su E_s	Wi E_s	Wi DE	Su E_s	Wi E_s	Wi DE	Su E_s	Wi E_s	Wi DE	Su E_s	Wi E_s	Wi DE	Su E_s
Job Complexity		-.10**				-.17**												-.23***			-.23***
Work Load																-.11**					-.20**
Role Ambiguity				+.10*										-.10*							-.15*
Underutilization of Abilities			+.13*																-.11**	-.09*	
Marital Stress									-.22***	-.08*											

*p < .10; **p < .05; ***p < .01

APPENDIX E. (Cont'd.)

Leavers at time 3.

Strains	Marital Dissatisfaction			Anxiety			Depression			Irritation			Somatic Complaints			Low Self-esteem			Job Dissatisfaction		
Social Supports / Stresses	Wi E_s	Wi DE	Su E_s	Wi E_s	Wi DE	Su E_s	Wi E_s	Wi DE	Su E_s	Wi E_s	Wi DE	Su E_s	Wi E_s	Wi DE	Su E_s	Wi E_s	Wi DE	Su E_s	Wi E_s	Wi DE	Su E_s
Job Complexity		-.12**							+.15**							-.09*					+.13*
Work Load				-.09*			-.11**			-.09*		-.15**	-.13***	-.09*							
Role Ambiguity	-.10**	+.09*							+.12*		+.10**	+.16**									-.13*
Underutilization of Abilities									-.13*						-.11*						-.19***
Marital Stress								-.10**	-.11*					-.12**							

*p< .10; **p <.05; ***p < .01

ISR RESEARCH REPORTS

The following Research Reports have been published by ISR. They are available in paperbound editions only. For information on prices and availability, write to the ISR Publishing Division, P.O. Box 1248, Ann Arbor, Michigan 48106.

Career Change in Midlife: Stress, Social Support, and Adjustment. John R. P. French, Jr., Steven R. Doehrman, Mary Lou Davis-Sacks, and Amiram Vinokur. 1983. 152 pp.

Compensating for Missing Survey Data. Graham Kalton. 1983. 164 pp.

Residential Displacement in the U.S., 1970-1977. Sandra J. Newman and Michael S. Owen. 1982. 98 pp.

Sex Role Attitudes among High School Seniors: Views about Work and Family Life. A. Regula Herzog and Jerald G. Bachman. 1982. 272 pp.

Subjective Well-Being among Different Age Groups. A. Regula Herzog, Willard L. Rodgers, and Joseph Woodworth. 1982. 115 pp.

Employee Ownership. Michael Conte, Arnold S. Tannenbaum, and Donna McCulloch. 1981. 70 pp.

Recreation and Quality of Urban Life: Recreational Resources, Behaviors, and Evaluations of People in the Detroit Region. Robert W. Marans and J. Mark Fly. 1981. 240 pp.

A Comparative Study of the Organization and Performance of Hospital Emergency Services. Basil S. Georgopoulos and Robert A. Cooke. 1980. 512 pp.

An Evaluation of "Freestyle": A Television Series to Reduce Sex-Role Stereotypes. Jerome Johnston, James Ettema, and Terrence Davidson. 1980. 308 pp.

Occupational Stress and the Mental and Physical Health of Factory Workers. James S. House. 1980. 356 pp.

Job Demands and Worker Health: Main Effects and Occupational Differences. Robert D. Caplan, Sidney Cobb, John R. P. French, Jr., R. Van Harrison, and S. R. Pinneau, Jr. 1980. 342 pp.

Perceptions of Life Quality in Rural America: An Analysis of Survey Data from Four Studies. Robert W. Marans and Donald A. Dillman, with the assistance of Janet Keller. 1980. 118 pp.

Social Support and Patient Adherence: Experimental and Survey Findings. Robert D. Caplan, R. Van Harrison, Retha V. Wellons, and John R. P. French, Jr. 1980. 283 pp.

Working Together: A Study of Cooperation among Producers, Educators, and Researchers to Create Educational Television. James S. Ettema. 1980. 220 pp.

Experiments in Interviewing Techniques: Field Experiments in Health Reporting, 1971-1977. Edited by Charles F. Cannell, Lois Oksenberg, and Jean M. Converse. 1979. 446 pp.

The 1977 Quality of Employment Survey: Descriptive Statistics, with Comparison Data from the 1969-70 and 1972-73 Surveys. Robert P. Quinn and Graham L. Staines. 1979. 364 pp.

The Physical Environment and the Learning Process: A Survey of Recent Research. Jonathan King, Robert W. Marans, and associates. 1979. 92 pp.

Results of Two National Surveys of Philanthropic Activity. James N. Morgan, Richard F. Dye, and Judith H. Hybels. 1979. 204 pp.

A Survey of American Gambling Attitudes and Behavior. Maureen Kallick, Daniel Suits, Ted Dielman, and Judith Hybels. 1979. 560 pp.